For the people of Lewis

THE HUB OF MY UNIVERSE

James Shaw Grant

Humour, Mystery, Tragedy and
Adventure from real life
in the Outer Hebrides...

Published by James Thin, 53-59 South Bridge, Edinburgh,
in collaboration with the author.

© James Shaw Grant 1982

ISBN 0 9508371 0 5

Printed in the Scottish Highlands by Nevisprint Limited, Fort William.

Contents

Author's Note

Three hundred years ago Sir Robert Gordon, who gave the world the first maps based on actual mensuration, wrote a Latin treatise (which I cannot read) identifying Lewis as Ultima Thule, the uttermost island of the Romans, on the very edge of their flat and saucerlike world.

So Lewis has remained to the inheritors of the Roman metropolitan arrogance — an island outwith their range of experience and therefore remote, romantic primitive and absurd.

I do not identify the inheritors of the Roman metropolitan arrogance. They will identify themselves if they read this book, just as they have frequently identified themselves in books and articles of their own.

This is written by a native who, after a lifetime's study, knows how little he knows. It is written primarily for Lewis people, for the friends all over the world with whom I have been in constant touch for more than half a century through the Stornoway Gazette.

I hope, however, that it will also be read by others. They may discover that there are two ends to a telescope and that hitherto they have been looking at the Outer Hebrides through the wrong one.

There will be other volumes to follow as my search for Lewis continues — always provided that the sales of this discharge my debt to the printers.

My debt to the people of Lewis will never be discharged.

This book is based on the reminiscences of the author and his father who between them reported the Hebridean scene from Stornoway for three quarters of a century. The author recalls the loss of H M Yacht Iolaire on New Year's Day 1919 with more than two hundred island servicemen going home on leave; the abortive attempt of the first Lord Leverhulme, the bouncy soap magnate, to industrialise Lewis and Harris; the greatest rescue by breeches buoy in the history of the sea and the thwarting of an attempt by an unscrupulous factor to cheat the widows and orphans of a Hebridean fishing disaster. He deals with social and cultural movements such as the passing of the great Gaelic story tellers; the struggle of an island community against a harsh environment and a remote bureaucracy; and the odd effects of prohibition on a thirsty town. He examines the effect of contemporary folklore on the life of a community. In an easy, almost conversational, way he moves from stories which hit the national headlines to amusing local incidents which are nevertheless of universal appeal. With a few simple phrases he conjures into life some of the outstanding characters in an island noted for its individuality. And he has a gift for the unexpected, as in the story of how a Lewis "Red Indian" saved the life of Charles Dickens's son, or how a tragic accident on a fishing boat in Stornoway harbour was "seen" in the tea leaves at an afternoon party as it was taking place.

1
Lovable Irrational Island

As soon as I try to define my own relationship to Lewis — the point of view from which I see the island — I come up against a difficulty.

I was born in Stornoway, and spent most of my working life there, but I feel that, in the full sense of the term, I am not a Lewisman, because I am not a Gaelic speaker, and that, despite the fact that I can trace my mother's family back in Lewis history, generation by generation, at least to 1600, and a good deal further in a more general way.

It is one of the peculiarities of Lewis that every native calls himself a Stornowegian, no matter where within the island he was born, but not every Stornowegian can claim to be an authentic Lewisman, an initiate of that intense freemasonry which enables a poor, remote and bleak Atlantic island to maintain an empire which comprehends the globe.

Lewis is a lovable, irrational island which confounds the facts of geography and sets at defiance the law of mathematics which asserts that the whole is greater than the part.

Stornoway seems to include Lewis and yet, in a sense, it is not itself authentically Lewisian.

I was born in a semi-detached house at the corner of Lewis Street and Scotland Street. A gaunt three-storeyed house with a lobby which was spacious out of all proportion to the rest, but as dark as a dungeon, with a row of pegs behind the front door on which there always hung a depressing assortment of hats and coats, including the cloth cap my father invariably wore (except on Sundays) although he was a professional man, an idiosyncrasy I have inherited from him just as surely as if it were predestined in my genes.

The house had no bathroom, but there was a w.c. in a sort of tunnel under the stair, with a bench-like wooden seat on which I once placed some of the sweets called jumbo balls — or jumba balls, as we pronounced it — in the strange belief that, if they were left there overnight, they would turn into money.

They didn't. Nothing ever turned into money in our family, although we were never poor, and never, I think, even conscious of the fact that we had less money than we could have used.

I can't remember who it was that persuaded me to experiment with the jumbo balls. So far as I know it was the only occasion on which I ever dabbled in magic, black or white, and I was never afraid of the supernatural, although Lewis at that time was still heavily infested with ghosts. As a young child I used to have to convoy one of my older playmates home when there was an aurora, because he thought it was the angels dancing.

When it came to physical bravery, however, it was very different. I can still recall the mixture of shame and stubborn pride with which I resisted the efforts of the

1

older boys to make me fight one of my classmates. Weight and reach were in my favour but I could see no point in fighting when I had no quarrel.

The older boys could enrage me, however, and frequently did, by chanting "Blood on your lip! Blood on your lip!" and pointing at me. I have no idea what the origin of the practice was, whether it was something personal to myself, or something other children were subject to, but once I turned on my tormentors, and pursued them out of the garden with stones so big they might have been lethal if my aim had been true.

I was never angrier in my life, and never happier. I often regret that, as I grew up, I lost the capacity for blind insensate rage. It is an effective, enjoyable, and, at times, a necessary purgative.

Although undistinguished architecturally the house was a solid one with a heavy iron railing round the front on top of a dwarf wall, and a heavy iron gate that never opened or shut. It always stood, immoveable, where it had sagged on the hinges and dug into the gravel, just sufficiently ajar to permit the passage of the family single file.

Also wide enough, of course, to permit the entry of the stray sheep which, in those days, roamed the streets of Stornoway in devouring bands, prospecting for anything green, or even remotely edible, with an appetite that was insatiable, and a cunning that passed belief.

The authorities at one time fitted a wicket gate at the school to keep the marauders out of the playground, but an old decrepit ewe stumbled on the secret and wandered in. Instead of making for the acres of grass spread temptingly before her, she went in and out the gate a dozen times as if memorising the secret or transmitting it to her tribe.

In a short time they were all in, spreading across the playground like a herd of buffaloes. The authorities abandoned the struggle and left the school gates wide.

Behind the house there was a walled garden, abandoned and reverting to wilderness. There were red currant and black currant bushes round the walls which were completely neglected but from which one could gather a few handfuls of fruit in season, and there was a square patch of gooseberry bushes which were of little use for anything except to snatch at our jerseys or trousers as we raced around.

The glory of the garden was a forest of rampant green rhubarb growing incongruously in a bed of cinders. The rhubarb was not ours. It belonged to the Maclennans who occupied the other half of the house.

Mrs Maclennan, the kindly ogress of my youth, fed her rhubarb diligently with the refuse from the fire, and it grew as mightily as the famous bean-stalk. Thick as a man's wrist, it thrust great green umbrellas aloft for little boys to crawl under and hide.

My father made an attempt to cultivate the garden once, during the first world war, but he had little leisure and less interest and, anyway, it was a losing fight.

When the sheep got in and savaged the flower bed which he had planted outside the dining room window, a neighbour asked, "Well, William, did the sheep eat your front?"

It became a humorous saying in the family, but in its origin it was not a solicitous enquiry. It was a rebuke. My father had refused to support the neighbour in a petition to the Town Council for the rigorous suppression of the strays.

I never asked my father why he would not sign the petition. He regarded the

2

sheep as a blight on the town just as surely as his neighbour did, but I suspect he had some sympathy for the crofters who owned them, and who were at that time too deeply involved with the Kaiser in Flanders, or Mesopotamia, or on the high seas, to know what their sheep were up to. Not that they bothered very much about the gardens when they were at home and did know!

Even if there had been no sheep there were Mrs Maclennan's hens!

They were unenclosed and uninhibited. They scrabbled in the seed beds. They squawked and scuttered beneath our feet at games. In summer, when we were allowed, for a few hot days, to shed our shoes in imitation of the hardier lads who were our heroes, we had to walk with care to avoid their little heaps of slimy dirt in unexpected places.

They even swaggered into the kitchen, if the door was left ajar. Nodding and pecking and messing the floor. And if there was nothing for them to eat it was only because our lunchtime fish, or meat, had already been sneaked away by their mortal enemy, Mrs Maclennan's mangy cat.

2
Fireships for the Fishermen

Mrs Maclennan was old, dark skinned, sharp featured, wrinkled. She dressed invariably in black, and spoke in a high pitched, raucous, penetrating voice. In appearance she was the archetypal witch, but there was nothing malevolent about her.

She was the very soul of generosity. A devout church goer. A lover of children and animals. But she was quite oblivious to dirt.

She had not the faintest perception of the effect her menagerie had on the neighbourhood, and particularly on my mother's nerves.

As a child I wandered into Mrs Maclennan's kitchen as freely as her hens, and I was just as welcome. I was liable at any moment to be offered a freshly baked pancake which had been laid to cool on the seat the cat had vacated, or a scone from a batch of baking which had been trodden by an agitated hen, shooed gently out of the way.

So far as I know, I never came to any harm as a result. My resistance to disease might have been strengthened by the early inoculation! The difficulties began when I was old enough to feel disgust, but still not suave enough to refuse her hospitality without offence.

In time I stopped going to Mrs Maclennan's kitchen, but her love pursued me into the garden, not with food but moral precepts.

I have long forgotten most of the Catechism, although it was dinned into me both at school and Sunday school, but I will never forget Mrs Maclennan's wagging finger and her sing-song admonition:

> *"It is a seen*
> *To steal a peen*
> *No less than any*
> *Greater theeng."*

For the first fifteen years of her married life my mother, a fastidious woman, endured this mixture of squalor and sanctimoniousness, and covered her feelings so well that it was only when I was a grown man I realised my childhood heaven had been her hell.

Once, when things threatened to get too much for her, she flung the fryingpan across the whitewashed kitchen with so much violence it knocked a piece of plaster from the wall. Afterwards, if she felt near the end of her tether, she looked at the hole and smiled.

It was probably the only emotional outburst of her married life, for she was a placid woman. She gave us almost complete liberty as children, and our friends had the run of the house. We could play in the dining room as freely as in the kitchen,

4

and even the best chairs could be commandeered if we wanted to make a railway train or ship.

But she could be strict when occasion demanded.

My brother and I quarrelled over a sling. It was a vicious implement with strong wooden frame and stout rubber thongs. It would throw a pebble an immense distance with considerable accuracy.

She told us once to settle our dispute. When we failed to do so, she took the sling, without a word, and stuffed it into the back of the fire.

She was afraid of it, I think, and glad of the excuse to destroy it, but I can still feel the desolation of our loss, and the sharp surprise that my mother could treat us so brusquely.

Mrs Maclennan's husband — and that is the right way to refer to him because she was the dominant — had suffered a mild stroke. He could still go out and about, and looked robustly healthy, but he could not speak.

We used to see him at an upstairs window watching our games with a restless, inquisitive eye. We never knew what he thought of our goings-on, but his disposition was friendly. If we met him on the street he pointed at us with his stick and went into a paroxysm of laughter.

After we had left the Lewis Street house, we used to meet him sometimes on a Sunday morning on our way to church, and wished that the street would swallow us up, before the pointing stick was raised in our direction, and the uncontrolled laughter rang out among the crowd.

He must have been able to hear, although not to speak, although that thought never occurred to me until now. Otherwise he would surely not have gone to church.

The Maclennans, just like ourselves, had to put up with a good deal for the sake of neighbourliness.

The horde of boys who played cowboys or football in the garden, who quarrelled and jumped and shouted, must have been a great source of annoyance to an elderly, ageing, childless couple. But they did not restrain us, and I cannot recall that any wrath descended on us even when the mangy cat died, and we buried it ceremonially in the garden, with a large tin can as a tombstone inscribed with white paint, "In unloving memory of the scabby cat."

The other neighbours were not all as forebearing. Indeed, when I think of all the people who at one time or another pursued me in anger, I am forced to conclude that I was anything but the simpering little angel the local photographer made me out to be.

There was Maggie Macneil, the saddler's daughter, who lived just across Scotland Street from us.

She was a brisk, competent, mannish person, who recited "Curfew Shall Not Ring Tonight" at Parish Kirk Socials, and who was said to have been seen tarring the roof of the garden shed, dressed in plus fours discarded by one of her lodgers, an eminent educationist with whom the more malicious of the local gossips, quite improbably, linked her name.

She must have had a fair degree of provocation the day she got our football in the garden, and drove a fork through it before she flung it back.

And Jonachan, fish salesman and coxswain of the lifeboat, who lived a little further down the street! It was not for love that he pursued us through the darkness,

5

in his bedroom slippers, without jacket or vest, holding his trousers precariously with one hand while he tried to grab us with the other.

I don't remember what the ploy was that night. We might have hung an ashbin on his door knob before we rang the bell. Or tied his door to the one across the street, than rang both bells together. Or it might have been "clockwork" — an empty pirn cut into a saw edge, and made to rattle on a window pane.

We may even have been smooring. A filthy habit in which a hollowed out cabbage stem was filled with oakum, and a live coal, to produce a thick, tarry smoke, which was then blown through a letter box or keyhole.

We had to make our own entertainments, and we did. Mostly at other people's expense. Although, personally, I never went as far as my second cousin, Willie Pope, who was of an older generation despite the relationship, and lived in Newton just across from the Patent Slip where ships were then built or repaired.

There was a privy down by the shore, which I remember well, although the slip was out of use in my day. It was just a shed, with a long wooden spar to sit on, and a long drop to the beach below, where, at high tide, the moving waters performed what the poet has called "their priestlike task of pure ablution round earth's human shores."

It was the custom, in the heyday of the yard, for the carpenters to sneak off to the privy in the morning for a quiet smoke, and a gossip, behind the foreman's back. Willie and one of his pals chose a day when the tide was out, sneaked in below them, and daubed the assembled bottoms with tar, hot from their own brazier.

A rather similar prank was played periodically by some of the older boys in my own day at the public convenience on the Steamer Quay — an ancient monument which should have been preserved as a memorial to the Point Street boys!

It was rather more efficient than the Newton privy, with a row of cubicles in which the pans were flushed automatically from a common cistern.

The boys would crowd into the cubicle nearest the cistern, and, when the waters began to move, they would drop in a burning newspaper, hoping that their fire ship would catch some fisherman or docker, at his devotions, further down the line.

It was a cowardly ploy because, in the circumstances, the culprits had plenty of time to escape — unlike my cousin Willie Pope who was too well known around the Slip to avoid suspicion, or escape retribution.

3
A House by the Shore

On Keith Street, the next street parallel to ours, there stood the ruins of a house. Just a few feet of wall at one end, opposite and close to, the door of a house that was still inhabited. Beyond that nothing but a tumbled mass of stones and nettles, and a little drying green at the back.

I never knew what happened to the old house. Whether it had been burnt. There was no evidence that I can remember of a fire. Or whether it had been a thatched house (of which there were still a few in town) which had been allowed to fall into decay. It did not look like that: the walls were too substantial.

Anyway as boys we were not interested in its history but in the uses we could put it to. We called it the Opening, and once I moved from the Lewis street garden into the wider world, this was my arena.

The games we played there were harmless enough for the most part. Football on the green, or on the street, often with a cork from a herring net for want of a ball. Or "leave-O" and "kick the can."

The last two provided plenty of high excitement in the darkness on a frosty night, but sometimes we got up to a more dangerous or less reputable ploy, such as terrifying the neighbours by exploding acetylene gas in a cocoa tin with a pin hole in the bottom, to which we daringly applied a match.

Or spying on courting couples, an occupation which must have been an irritant to the quarry, but at which we never saw much. We had to draw on our own licentious, but ill-informed, imaginations, for the titillation that we sought.

Even in the derelict Opening we were involved in war on three fronts, and some of the trouble was not of our making.

A butcher, whom we knew as Ian Chuil, disputed our right to be there at all. So far as I know we had just as much right to play football on the green as he had to graze his cow, but he had a hay fork and we had none. He also had a fiery temper which exercised our fleetness of foot.

Many years later I discovered that Ian Chuil was really a kindly old man. A very much younger cousin of mine, on holiday from England, became his friend and his pet, tolerated and fussed over. In one way it was a pleasant surprise, but in another it was a shock. A guilty shock. We might have been the aggressors after all! On the other hand it may be that the old man had mellowed.

On the other side was a shopkeeper whom I knew only as Captain. I have no idea what his surname was, or whether he had ever been a captain, but he probably had been a seafaring man, and certainly he had been abroad.

When he was in a good mood he used to describe for us the beggars in some port he visited whose invariable refrain, according to Captain, was, "No fadder! No mudder! No sister! No brudder! and hungry beleee!"

These cordial moods were rare and he spent most of his time chasing us from the

7

vicinity of the shop with a hook designed for lifting down the hams he stored suspended from the ceiling. It was a weapon every bit as dangerous as Ian Chuil's hayfork, but I don't think we came to any harm.

The lady who lived beside the Opening, close to the derelict house, had more to complain of. She was a prim little spinster whom we called Eesa. I presume her name was Isa.

She was a great friend of my auntie Jessie, but family feeling was no protection when she came bounding from the front door to chase us away. Our noise and clamour, so close to her window, must have been a real annoyance, and we tormented her still further by running no faster than was necessary to keep beyond her reach.

If by chance she seized our ball, we stood at a safe distance and made faces until she lost her temper and threw it at us.

The horse drawn lorries, the carts and the traps which thronged Cromwell Street — a quite improbable but highly significant name! — seldom penetrated to our part of the town. And a motor car was a rarity. We would run a mile to see one.

In spite of the various harassments which added to the excitement of our existence, we had freedom. Complete freedom! Of the gardens, and the streets, and each other's houses. Of the quays, and the fields, and the Castle Grounds.

And also of the Cockle Ebb, where we used to go on sunny Saturdays. Through the gate of Goathill Farm. Down by the spring where we always stopped to drink the ice cold water. Past the bull park, where despite the wall and fence, we covered every patch of red we wore. And on to the saltings where there was a graveyard for horses whose bones were exposed by the tide in shallow pits of sand, surrounded by green sea grass and myriads of pinks.

And so out to the beach where tell-tale marks in the sand told us where to dig for cockles. Or into the river where, on the flowing tide, you could catch small flounders beneath your feet.

There are few sensuous pleasures in life to compare with the thrill a small boy gets when he feels a lively flounder wriggling beneath his toes.

Though I enjoyed these expeditions I was always a solitary observer of life rather than a doer, and a great deal of my time was spent standing in doorways timidly watching the weaver, or the blacksmith who worked quite close to us, or the joiner at the far end of the street.

I must have been on friendly terms with the joiner because I was privileged to wade through the knee-deep shavings and stir the glue-pot for him.

I dare say the blacksmith would have welcomed me too, but I always stood well back from the sparks when he hammered a piece of glowing iron, and I was very cautious in approaching the smiddy at all if there was a horse outside the door waiting to be shod, though I loved the pungent smell of burning when the hot shoe sizzled on the upraised hoof.

The weaver's shed was very dark and one went down a step to it. The floor was cobbled with large round pebbles from the beach, and the loom was an old fashioned one with heavy bars which he kicked with his feet, and a leather thong at each side with which he threw the shuttle back and fore. Even at that time, although I did not speak Gaelic, I called him the breabadair. I did not know until much later how apt the name was!

On wet days, and they were frequent, we played in our attic, or in the attic of my cousin and closest companion, Stephen MacLean.

Our attic was gloomy with only a sky-light, while Stephen's was bright with a view over the houses lower down, right to the Town Hall Clock and Gallows Hill. But ours was the favourite. It was roomier, and it had physical features around which we could deploy our mighty armies.

There was a bed with an old straw mattress as hard as the rock of Gibraltar, a brown metal trunk, and a wooden tea box covered with green and red flowered wall paper, and reeking of some sickly scent spilt in it years before by a long departed maid who had used it as a dressing table.

We could not afford tin soldiers, and our armies consisted of hundreds of multi coloured tramway tickets brought to us from Glasgow by friends.

Once, when I was about ten, and Stephen a good eighteen months younger, we set up a publishing business in the attic, each producing a newspaper which we wrote in big childish script on the back of red and blue handbills which Stephen's father got from the C.P.R. to advertise assisted passages for emigrants to Canada.

I don't remember how long the craze lasted, or what we wrote, but when we ran out of steam, Stephen solved the problem by filling the whole of one issue, from the title to the imprint, with the bold announcement, "Owing to pressure on our space all the usual features have been crowded out".

The only pressure on the space was his own announcement!

4
Seaport Town with a Busy Harbour

Of all the activities that occupied the eleven years I spent in Lewis Street, the one that took most time and gave most pleasure, as I remember it, was grinding broken flower pots with a discarded window weight.

It seems an aimless sort of pastime, and I am puzzled to know why it appealed to me so much. Looking back I seem to have spent not only hours, but weeks and months, outside the kitchen window, patiently beating the shards into a satisfying red dust.

I can better understand the hours I spent in my grannie's house in Newton, alone in the little bedroom above the porch, with my nose to the window, watching the grey seas scudding in before a southerly gale until they were frustrated by the island that divided the bay.

On clear days you could see the hills of Wester Ross marching along the horizon thirty miles across the Minch, but I preferred the storms with rain lashing on the window, and a mad dance of breakers on the shore.

There was no causeway in those days linking Goat Island to the shore and, incidentally, sheltering the houses along the sea front. When the tide was in with a southerly gale, the seas splashed over the top of the house. It was impossible to use the front door at all and even coming in through the garden from Kipper Road, one got a flurry of salt spray on the face.

On one occasion I was sent to Cameron's shop at the corner of Newton Street and Island Road with a five pound note. I was only a child, and as I grappled with the sneck of the shop door, the wind whipped the note from my hand and it vanished down the street.

I raced back to my grannie's blubbering over the loss. A five pound note in those days was a modest fortune. My aunts went scurrying along the street with little hope of retrieving it. But they did!

Just about the spot where the causeway now joins the street the £5 note was pinned to the ground by a stream of water from a friendly "gok" which someone had forgotten to turn off. Cameron as I remember him was a quiet-spoken, friendly, sandy-haired man. An ex-navyman or ex-coastguard, I think.

Many years later, when Colin Cameron, a Stornoway businessman, established a knitwear shop in the old High Street of Edinburgh, I went in to make a purchase. I asked if Mr Cameron was in.

"Do you know Mr Cameron?" asked the shop assistant.

"I should hope so," I replied. "I used to do business with his grandfather."

She looked a little startled.

It is my belief that every boy should be born in a seaport town, with a busy harbour, but no traffic on the streets. He should have an indulgent mother who doesn't fuss when he comes home late. He should live in a northern latitude where

10

the seasons range from the blackness of winter to the endless twilight of June, and the rain and the sun and the frost and the gales and the aurora borealis follow each other in such bewildering succession that no day is like the one before it or the one which will come after it, but every one is rich with its own experience.

And he must have a grannie with a house by the shore, with an old brass telescope through which you can watch the ships and try to tell by the flags whether they are Norwegian or Swedish or German or Russian, and huge shells brought home from some tropical climate by her sailor husband, in which you can hear the roar of distant seas.

And a little celluloid mannikin with lead in the ball on which he stands, so that he keeps you amused for hours on end by refusing to lie flat when you push him over.

And a little bottle of scent inside an imitation bun. And a huge ram's horn on the flagstones in the porch which you can hold to your head and pretend you are a bull charging, or to your mouth, and pretend you are a trumpeter.

And a little china pig which you can clumsily drop on the floor, exclaiming in all innocence, "the piggy neary boke", as you gaze at the shattered fragments of one of the household gods.

I was back and fore from Newton from my earliest childhood, in convoy with the family so to speak. Indeed there is still an argument as to whether it was I or my brother who made the childishly profound observation on a winter night, "There's a moon in Newton too," surprised that the lower part of the town should be as well provided for as Lewis Street.

From a very early age I was also free to wander round the quays, alone or with my pals. In fact the quays were the playground of Stornoway in those days. A playground which no modern facilities can ever equal.

We had a maid for a short time who used to take me for a walk in the afternoon before I won my freedom. I cannot recall her name or even her appearance. But I can remember the dim, crowded interior of her mother's house in Shell Street where she dragged me one day and left me swinging my legs on a high mahogany chair with a horse-hair seat while she and her mother gossiped.

It happened only once. I rebelled, and my mother, after due inquiry, upheld my complaint. Thereafter I was free to organise my own excursions.

We spent a lot of time as boys fishing from the "slants" — the wooden slipways which existed in those days underneath the piers by which small boats could be hauled above high water mark.

As we grew more daring we clambered down the iron ladders to the cross beams of the wharf, and fished from there, or made our way from point to point, swinging precariously round the greenheart piles, from one beam to the next, with the sea below and the townsfolk promenading overhead.

Once, having got to a cross beam at a point where there was no ladder, by clambering up from a fishing boat, two of us were trapped when the boat unexpectedly put to sea. The beams were so close together we could not even stand erect. I cannot recall how we eventually made our escape.

It is surprising there were so few accidents. I cannot recall a single fatality among the lads I played with around the piers, although there were occasional drowning accidents when boys were swimming in other places.

I once fell into the sea, but that was at Newton in full view of my grannie's house. Within earshot too!

11

I was walking along a sewer cased in concrete which carried the offal from the kipper sheds out below low-water mark. Or was supposed to! The part of the pipe between the tide marks was green and slimy with seaweed, and I shot off it into a few inches of water. I was never in any danger, but I was wet and miserable, and my dignity was hurt. I shouted for help, and lay kicking my heels in the air until someone dragged me out.

Stephen had a more serious escapade when he fell from Cromwell Street Quay into deep water. I wasn't with him at the time, but I learned afterwards that he got out, partly by his own efforts, although he could not swim, and partly by the help of an older lad who was with him — Louis Bain, who lived across the wall from us in Lewis Street, and later had a distinguished career in the Colonial service.

These escapades did not deter us from spending our time in dangerous places, fishing for cuddies and bodach-ruadhs, mackerel and caravanochs, and every summer, on the day the school closed, we made a ceremonial pilgrimage to the harbour to sail our jotters out to sea, leaf by leaf, folded into paper boats.

No monarch ever looked on his armada with greater pride, or saw it disappear beyond the horizon with greater pleasure.

A whole year's schooling, drifting away, leaving us free for seven glorious weeks.

5
Storms from the Western Ocean

My father was the local observer for the Meteorological Office. It was one of the many chores he did to eke out his meagre earnings as local correspondent for the Highland News, which was the only weekly effectively serving Lewis at that time.

There were no weather ships in those days, let alone satellites, and Stornoway was one of the five main weather stations. They were strategically chosen to give warning of storms coming in from the Western Ocean.

We had a Stevenson screen in the garden with four thermometers — dry, wet, maximum and minimum. There was a rain gauge as well, but the sunshine recorder was in a garden behind the Masonic Lodge where the horizon was freer from obstruction.

In the dining room there were two mercury barometers and an aneroid barograph. Once a week I was privileged to see my father put a new "pinny" on the barograph, when he removed the old chart for forwarding to London and put on a new one.

As well as the official service my father sent weather telegrams to the Daily Telegraph and the German Government. These services came to an abrupt end in 1914 when war broke out, and I was given the discarded books of Telegraph passes to play with. I cherished them for years, and I still have the "Admiral Fitzroy Storm Barometer" which the Daily Telegraph presented to my father when weather reports were banned.

The instruments were read several times a day, and coded messages were sent to the Met. Office in London, giving the rise or fall in atmospheric pressure, the wind direction and force, the temperature, humidity, rainfall, cloud formation and amount.

One day at lunch my father noticed a dramatic drop in the purple line traced by the barograph pen. There was nothing to account for it in the weather outside. Although it was not the time for a reading to be taken he decided to send a special telegram to London.

That was the first warning the Met Office had of a violent blizzard coming in from the north west. In a short time the whole of Britain, and most of northern Europe, was blanketed by snow. Later my father was told that, as a result of his warning, the Royal Flying Corps — as it then was — had been grounded, while the German air force suffered serious loss.

I was too young at the time to have any direct recollection of that particular blizzard. I know of it by hearsay and it is inextricably mixed up in my memory with another, which struck the island on a Sunday night some years later.

My father and mother were at church. My brother and I were reading at the dining room table by the light of an oil lamp, when the snow crept up on us unawares.

For some odd reason, although the house was comparatively new, and Stornoway had had a mains supply of gas for nearly half a century, there was no gas in the house. The owner must have been very conservative or parsimonious, or both.

That was before the days even of the Tilley or the Aladdin, but although its range was limited the old wick lamp gave a warm, embracing light. To sit within its circle with a book was to be in fairy land.

But that night we were worried. Our parents did not come home at the usual time, nor for long after it. When they did arrive the reason was clear. They were white from head to foot. The blizzard had been so severe at the time the churches were due to skail the congregations had to stay on until the blizzard moderated.

A snow fall like that was of little use to us as children. The drifts were too deep. What we liked was a thin covering of snow which we could beat into ice with our bonnets to make a slide on which a constant stream of boys would follow each other on their tackety boots.

As soon as I was tall enough to peer into the Stevenson screen I was trained to take the readings, but when I was too young for that, my task was to take the telegrams to the Post Office, or, during the war, to the Admiral's Office in the old Imperial Hotel which later became the Louise Carnegie Girls' Hostel.

In charge of the naval base was Admiral Tupper who had a secretary named Crowe. For some odd reason the Admiral insisted on addressing him as Mr Rook. At last the worm turned. One morning when the Admiral barked out his customary, "Mr Rook!" Mr Crowe replied, "Yes, Admiral Putter."

It was a shrewd hit. The Admiral was a golf addict. He gifted the Tupper Cup to the Stornoway Club which was played for annually for many years, and may still be, although I have a feeling that someone won it thrice in succession and successfully claimed permanent possession.

One evening, it must have been shortly after the end of the war — I was on my way to the Post Office when I fell in with some older boys who were going out to see a battleship lying just off the lighthouse.

Instead of going home for tea when my mission to the Post Office was accomplished, I joined them. The sailors invited us aboard and showed us through the ship. As darkness fell we came home jubilant, each with a huge slab of navy cocoa. It was almost black in colour and as hard as mahogany, but we ate it like chocolate. It was hard, harsh, unsweetened, but ambrosial.

Stornoway was regularly visited by battleships in those days, and even much later. The arrival of a ship was always a great occasion, marked generally by a football match against the visiting team, and a golf match. And quite frequently by a concert in the evening.

The best concerts I attended as a youngster were naval concerts sustained by a visiting ship's company. It was one way of returning the hospitality extended to the vessel by the townsfolk.

In a period earlier than I can recall Stornoway was sometimes visited by the whole of the Channel fleet, and for days on end the navy took over the town.

The loss of Stornoway's naval base was a considerable disaster. It diminished the status of the town. It also meant that the hundreds of Lewis reservists now had to travel to Chatham or Portsmouth for their training, instead of getting it within their own island, where they spent their money within the local economy.

The economic loss to the community must have been quite severe, and there were other losses less tangible but not less real. I was not, however, interested in that at the time. The navy was important only for the excitement it added to the day.

The cinema, television, or organised games in the most splendid surroundings, is a poor substitute for a busy harbour to a growing boy.

We had all the fresh air and exercise we could take, and there was hardly a moment of the day when our minds were not quickened by the arrival or departure of a vessel of some kind.

Stornoway was then in its hey day as a herring port. The season lasted for ten months out of the twelve. The longest herring fishing season of any port in Europe.

In early May the drifters would begin to arrive from Wick, Buckie, Banff and Peterhead — even from Lowestoft.

Smaller boats would come across the Minch from Broadford and Kyle or up from the Clyde.

And there was our own local fleet of S.Y.'s. We were S.Y.'s ourselves in the local parlance, and the registration letters of the fishing boats, BRD or BCK or PD or LT, was the first intimation I had that I belonged to a people apart, an island race, quite different from the Buckochs, or the Sassunaich, or even the Gaelic-speaking BRD's from the neighbouring island of Skye.

6
Too Young to Run a Cinema

By early June when the matje, or maiden, herring from the Minch were the best in the world, fetching fabulous prices in markets from Hamburg and Danzig to New York, there would be three or four hundred drifters and motor boats working out of Stornoway, with a sprinkling of sailing boats, which we referred to as whurries — presumably a corruption of wherry.

The drifters cast a pall of black smoke over the town. The chug-chug-chug of the motor boats could be heard a long way from the harbour when the fleet put out to sea in the late afternoon. But it was the slow silent progress of the whurries with their brown lugsails which caught our hearts, as they tacked back and fore in the enclosed waters of the bay, inching their way to the open sea.

Sometimes in a calm they had to be rowed out with long sweeps which the men worked standing on the deck. A laborious time consuming task, but a rare sight if you were idly watching from the pier with nothing to do but try to sink a bottle or a can by throwing stones at it, or to sneak a few herring from an unattended barrel to make bait for your line.

The names of the boats were music, and we knew them all. A litany which ran through our daily conversation.

The Herring Fisher. The Ellen and Irene. The Provider. The Comrade. The Muirneag. The Bure. The Paradigm. Even *The Ichthyology.* That was one way of learning to spell!

They lay in the harbour each Saturday and Sunday banked four or five deep from the piers. During the week they were always on the move. Coming or going. Discharging their catches. Or crossing the harbour to queue at the hulks in Glumaig Bay for bunkers.

From time to time each morning, as a latecomer crept into harbour with a cloud of gulls overhead, and her bows well down, betokening a heavy catch, one of the fish salesmen would come to the door of the odd pagoda-shaped fish mart, ringing a hand bell. The curers, hearing the call, would hurry back from their offices, or from some distant part of the pier, where they were superintending the landing of their earlier purchases.

Their first task was to study a sample of the newcomer's catch, and assess its quality.

The samples were set out for this purpose in a scoop, or tray, on a high stand. The scoop was hinged and when the sale was completed the sample was tipped back into one of the ship's baskets where it was held until the whole cargo was discharged in case there was a dispute.

There was plenty of room for dispute when a score or so of herring had to be selected to give an indication of the distribution of large, medium and small fish in a whole cargo, as well as the varying condition of the fish, as they fattened up with the progress of the season, or suddenly became thin and miserable spents when their biological function was discharged.

The fishermen and the curers looked at the catch from very different points of view. Not only were the interests of buyer and seller directly antagonistic, the fisherman compared his catch with the catch he had yesterday, or the day before, while the curer was concerned with the particular market into which he was selling, and the price he was likely to get a week or even a month ahead.

There was a long row of these sample scoops in the fish mart with the names of the different salesmen along the backs. Behind them was a broad wooden dais which served sometimes as a seat, but more often as a vantage point for the salesman, or for a curer who had come late and had to peer over shoulders to see the catch.

Once the sale began the curers, or kipperers, would bid with the flick of an eyelid, or an almost imperceptible movement of a pipe. The auctioneer, missing not the slightest movement in the crowd, would knock it down to the highest bidder, whose signal only he had identified — perhaps a hundred thousand herring in a single transaction.

Stretched out around the pier for nearly a mile were the curers' stances, where women in brightly coloured blouses and headscarves, with heavy boots and leather or rubber aprons, bloodied to the elbow with herring offal, and with their fingers bandaged to cover the cuts they had already received or protect them from those that were still to come, gutted the herring with incredible speed, and flung each fish behind them with unerring aim, although they never turned to look, into one of three or four wooden buckets, according to its size and grade.

Down in the Newton district of the town hundreds more worked under cover, splitting herring for kippering, hanging them on tenterhooks on large frames for the men to hoist into high kilns over smouldering fires of oak chips, which cast a blue smoke over the whole town.

The smoke filled our lungs with a rich aromatic odour which was pleasant in itself, and carried with it the prospect of kippers for breakfast. Succulent Minch kippers, completely free from dye or any colouring except oak smoke, fat enough to fry in their own juice, and sweeter in their unadorned simplicity than any dish contrived by a chef.

But that is now little more than a memory. The greed of the processors, substituting dye for smoke, first destroyed the kipper. Then the greed of the fishermen, substituting the purse seine for the drift net, almost completely destroyed the herring itself. A shameful story! But even in memory a Stornoway kipper is a sheer delight.

There was no motor traffic in the town, or very little, but scores of carters from the Laxdale district — little men with long moustaches and a taste for liquor, — drove like Jehus through the town towards Newton, along streets known to the Post Office as James Street and Bells Road, but known to the boys who had changed the nameplates as Jam Street and Hell Road.

In the height of the fishing season their wheels churned the waterbound clay into a thick black porridge, laced liberally with oil from the herring which fell from the barrels as they clattered along. So deep was the mud at times that on a Sunday, when I was going to visit my grannie with my best shoes on, I had to be carried across the street.

The first sign of the approaching herring season was the beaching of boats on the sand in front of the Caledonian Hotel for scraping and repainting.

About the same time cargoes of coal arrived to replenish the hulks, but this was a distant transaction on the far side of the bay, with which we boys were not much concerned except when we could borrow a rowing boat and go prospecting.

Then cargoes of rough salt arrived from Runcorn or Spain to be poured on the quay in heaps like gritty discoloured snow. Mountains of empty barrels also appeared on the quays — fresh, clean virgin timber, not yet soiled by oozing brine and oil and fat. And great masses of thin timber boards from East coast yards, or direct from Scandinavia, for making kipper boxes.

Some of my friends worked every evening after school making boxes at so much a dozen, or went round the piers picking up herring as they fell from the baskets hoisted aloft from the holds of the drifters.

They laced the herring through the gills with string to make a "gad" and sold them round the houses. Prime fresh herring, straight from the sea, at sixpence a score.

I was not allowed to work at the boxes, or "cadge" herring round the town, but once, when I was four or five, I went with my friend and neighbour Davy Sime to apply for work as projectionists at the cinema, which was then on Keith Street where the Carlton is today.

An amused and astonished manager told us to come back when we were a little older!

A few months later the picture house caught fire, and it gave me a certain satisfaction to watch the blaze from a window diagonally across the street — the home of the Smalls.

Small was a solicitor. Mrs Small was a huge rombustious kindly Irishwoman who belied her surname both physically and mentally. Her maiden name was even more inappropriate. Before she became Mrs Small she had been Miss Meek. Their son, Roland, was one of my playmates.

More than half a century after the destruction of the picture house, one of the delegates at a conference in Edinburgh, organised by the Scottish Country Industries Development Trust, of which I was then a member, surprised me by remarking that he had been born in Stornoway.

He was a son of Freer, the man who thought I was too young at five to run his cinema.

7
Stornoway Herring and the Red Revolution

The Stornoway herring fishing was already in difficulties when I knew it first, although that was by no means obvious, and the record years for volume of catch were still to come.

In 1917 there were 75,000 barrels of herring lying on the pier and in the yards at Stornoway, deteriorating under rain and sun, because the government refused permission to export them.

The matter was solemnly debated in the House of Commons.

"Really we must have pickled herrings", quipped the Speaker, and the government insisted that we needed them for food at home in war time.

When, at last, after months of argument, it penetrated the official mind that the herring had been hard cured for the Russian market, and were quite unacceptable to British palates, even in war time, they let the consignment go.

The herring might just as well have rotted on the pier. The Russian Revolution came along, and they were never paid for.

At political meetings in Stornoway, well into the twenties, portly fish-curers with watch chains and amber pendants slung across their paunches, would ask aggressively, but without much hope, what this party or the other intended to do about the Russian debts.

They could afford the losses at the time. There had been other pickings in the war. But the lean years which followed ruined some of them, and drove others into quite different enterprises.

From 1924 to 1928 Stornoway had an extraordinary run of heavy fishings. After the normal summer season unusually heavy shoals moved into the lochs.

You could sometimes hear the great mass of fish swimming through the water. In some of the villages along Loch Erisort it was possible to fill a bucket with herring direct from the shore.

In the winter of 1927, in a space of six weeks, the fleet working out of Stornoway took thirty million herring from Loch Erisort alone.

But if our eyes had been open we could have seen, even then, the writing on the wall.

None of these great catches came near the port of Stornoway. They were loaded in the loch straight into "klondykers", where they were lightly roused with salt, and taken direct to Germany to be made into Bismarcks or processed in some other way.

So, on the continent, and especially in Scandinavia, new methods of preserving herring were developed, and the shore trade of Stornoway and other Scottish ports began to dwindle.

In effect the Scottish fleet became a mere supplier of raw material for more enterprising manufacturers elsewhere.

The decline in the Scottish herring fishery was initiated by the conservatism of the processors who shied away from new products and new marketing techniques. Paradoxically it was completed by the haste with which the fishermen embraced new technology without regard to the critical point at which efficiency and conservation became incompatible.

The name "klondyker" was derogatory. It implied that the trawlers and cargo vessels which came from Germany to load up with herring were going for a quick buck. Perhaps they were, but the name itself should have warned us that they were working a gold mine which we ignored.

Stornoway did, indirectly, draw some benefit from the klondyking boom. I have heard it said, and I have no reason to doubt it, that, as the sales which took place at sea went through the salesmen's books, harbour dues were collected on them although the herring had never been near the port.

And for a few lively winters during my boyhood we had the unusual experience of welcoming the New Year twice in the same night.

In those days we did not sit in front of the telly waiting for big Ben to usher in the new year. The signal came from the vessels in the harbour sounding their sirens, and a joyous noise they could make when the harbour was busy. We used to lie in bed in Lewis Street and try to identify some of the participants like *the Sheila, the Glendun* or *the Glentaise.*

During the klondyking boom the first new year arrived by German time and the second, an hour later, by British time.

It was earlier even than the klondyke days, however, that an inebriated Lewisman was heard announcing, as he staggered along Cromwell Street, "This is mahogany night. The last night of the world!"

The West Coast fishing took another knock when the government exposed the winter fishing to the full blast of Norwegian competition in a deal for the export of coal.

This cynical sacrifice of the north west of Scotland for the sake of the north east of England had far reaching results. Without the winter fishing in the Minch, the Scottish herring fleet was unable to make full use of its capital investment, and a steady decline in the number of boats set in.

Less than twenty years after the peak year for landings at Stornoway, when more than 200,000 crans were netted, a government committee, presided over by an eminent Scot, an ex-Secretary of State in fact, was able to write a report on the Scottish herring fishery without even mentioning that there was a winter season.

His plans for the future were based on the assumption that the fleet would be engaged in herring fishing for less than half the year.

The folly was compounded by the fact that, by the time the report was published, the winter fishing was again being prosecuted in the Minch, which had become an important source of protein for beleagured Britain in the Hitler war. But now the herring were required for the home market, and the bulk of the catch was landed at mainland markets and taken straight to the consumer.

It was around that time that a well known Lewisman, Louis Bain, fell foul of the law for doing an eminently sensible thing.

He had arranged with a firm of kipperers in Greenock to supply them with herring. Part of each catch was gutted before being despatched from Stornoway so that they could go straight into the kippering kiln at Greenock while the rest of the catch was being prepared. In this way the throughput was practically doubled. An important saving in war time.

But the Ministry of Food had fixed a price for whole herring: not for gutted. The consequence was that Louis Bain was taken to court for contravening the price regulations and savagely fined.

A few weeks later the Ministry saw sense and amended the regulation. But the fine was not repaid.

The same set of regulations, working in the opposite way led to Lewis fish hawkers being fined for selling whole haddock retail. Haddock were supposed to be gutted by the wholesaler and the offal used for fish meal. The Ministry was not prepared to accept that "ceann cropic" was a better use for fish livers than sending them to the Gut House.

As almost all the Lewis fishermen were in the R.N.R., mobilised before war was actually declared, the anomalous situation arose that the great natural wealth of the Minch was tapped almost exclusively by stranger boats, and the only benefit which the adjacent communities derived was a little dock labour in Gairloch and Ullapool, loading the lorries before they headed south.

Even before the war, the newly formed Herring Industry Board delivered a body blow to Stornoway by closing the port at the start of the Yarmouth season to make a better market for the North Sea catch.

I protested at the time, in a leader, that it was rather like banning Cox's Orange Pippins in an effort to create a market for wizened crabs.

As a result of all these forces Stornoway practically died as a fishing port in the years immediately after the second world war, but a decade later a revival began, thanks to the generosity of a man who left Lewis without a penny in his pocket, and with hardly a word of English, but who never forgot the island in which he had been nurtured.

8
Gin I were a Baron's Heir

Even in its hey-day the herring fishing was uncertain. Heavy landings alternated with storms when fishing was impossible, or with blank spells when the shoals seemed to disappear.

There were no echo-sounders in those days. Shoals were traced by the appearance of the water or the activity of sea birds. However skilled a skipper was in reading the signs, there was a big element of hit and miss.

I remember one occasion, I think it must have been just before the second world war, when the Stornoway fleet returned to port empty handed day after day, except for one Lowestoft boat which regularly secured good catches. Even when the other boats fishing from the port, East Coast as well as local, tried to stalk him and fish the same waters, he got fish and they got none.

Eventually it was discovered that, acting on a hunch, he was setting his nets much deeper in the water than normal.

Nowadays the fisherman can see the shoal before he bothers to set a net, and attempts are being made to measure the temperature of the sea by remote sensors using satellites. As temperature seems to be a determining factor in the movement of the shoals, the fisherman, in future will know where the fish are going before they get there. If there are any fish at all left for him to catch!

The fishing fleet was like a dry tide, a wooden tide, whose movements were much more dramatic than those of the sea, and regulated by the calendar and the clock rather than the moon.

Around lunch time, in the height of the season the harbour would be full of boats, heaped up, as it were, around the quays. A few hours later the harbour would be empty, but a pall of smoke covering many square miles would mark the progress of the busy armada, hurrying back to sea.

Sometimes all the drifters would head in the same direction because heavy shoals had been located in a particular area. More often the fleet divided. Some heading south towards the Shiant Islands. Some north to Sandy Bay or Rhuda Reidh or the Butt of Lewis, or even the waters round North Rona or the Flannans.

On one or two rare occasions in winter the herring came right into Stornoway Harbour, and one could see the fleet at work within a few cables of the shore, hauling hundreds of thousands of herring in full view of the Fish Mart.

So many nets were set in the harbour one season the mail steamer could not put to sea for fear of fouling her propellers. The town was cut off from the mainland and business men were up in arms.

In the end, the Harbour Commissioners had to promote a Parliamentary Order giving them the power to prohibit the setting of nets within the harbour limits.

Normally the fleet had long distances to steam in search of shoals, and anxious eyes watched in the morning as they returned to port, seeking to gauge whether the fleet was heavily or lightly fished.

All the boats did not return together, because they came from widely separated fishing grounds, and, while one section of the fleet might have struck it lucky, another might be blank.

The kipperers and curers had to make up their minds whether to buy early irrespective of the price, because herring were going to be scarce that day, or hold off until late in the morning in the hope of a glutted market.

Large staffs might be standing idle with nothing to do for days, or even weeks, if the fishing failed, but a lucky strike would have everyone working till midnight by the light of kerosene flares.

On these occasions the harbour front looked like something out of Dante's Inferno, with the flickering lights mounted on upended kits, and the shadowy movement of the fishergirls round the farlins, and the coopers with their hammers, sealing the barrels by putting on the topmost hoop.

When the fishergirls had nothing to do they could be seen marching through the town, half a dozen in a row, often with their arms linked, singing. Or in ones and twos, talking and knitting. If there were no herring to gut there were still stockings to make for husbands and boy friends. They were never idle, and, although it was a life of great physical hardship, they were never dull.

In the fish market the uncertainties of the trade produced its own philosophy of life. The curers and salesmen for the most part were generous, boisterous, full of fun, with the gambler's readiness to accept the luck of the day just as it came.

I have seen a kipperer, John Woodger, I think it was, making quite a substantial windfall in a morning just because a long distance call from the continent took him out of the market when the catch looked like being small, and his rivals were paying famine prices.

By the time his call was over there were several boats coming into port with more than a hundred crans apiece, and he picked up his day's requirements dirt cheap.

I have known a cargo of cured herring appreciate in value several fold in the course of a voyage from Stornoway to Hamburg.

They were being exported by Charlie Alexander. He told me he had no market for them and would have to put them into cold store at considerable cost. But a sudden collapse of the East Anglian fishing left the market short, and he sold the whole cargo as soon as the vessel discharged it.

When times were slack the curers and salesmen played bezique or poker in each other's offices. One of them was reputed to know every card by the back. On one occasion a disgusted opponent threw his cards on the table declaring, "You have the devil's own luck. When you go to hell you'll find ice!"

On other occasions they organised competitions, fishing cuddies like the kids. Quite unaware that they were anticipating one of the up-market pastimes of the future — sea angling.

Or they would sit on the ledge of one of the market windows and sing popular ballads with great gusto in a strange assortment of accents, with the guttural Scoto-Flemish of the Moray Firth, and the broad dialect of East Anglia, dominating the soft West Highland drawl.

At times they got involved in some more elaborate ploy like setting up Johnny Toe, a kenspeckle figure around the town, in business as a fish hawker.

23

They provided him with an extravagant barrow and even opened a bank account for him, until the whole town knew what was afoot and we drove our singing teacher crazy by bawling out our own version of "Molly Malone".

In Storn'way's fair city
Where the girls are so pretty,
I first met my loved one,
The sweet Johnny Toe,
As he wheeled his wheel barrow
Through streets broad and narrow,
Crying herring, fresh herring,
A shilling the score.

Many years later, when Stornoway was at its lowest ebb as a fishing port, one of the old Fish Market "choir" lay dying.

Some of his cronies went to see him, not with conventional condolences, but with a bottle of whisky. When they had polished it off, the invalid got out of bed in his nightshirt and saw them to the top of the stair, where they all joined, for the last time, in a rousing rendition of "Gin I were a Baron's Heir", which had been the pride of their repertoire.

9
Two Anthems to One God

The fishermen were quite a different breed from the curers and fish salesmen.

They lived with physical danger as well as the gamble of the markets, and they were intensely, emotionally religious.

At the week-ends the Lewis fishermen disappeared into the landscape, as it were, returning to their home villages, but the Moray Firth men remained on their boats.

Revivals were common and it was not unusual to see a large crowd gathered in Perceval Square on a Saturday evening round the old ornamental fountain which was melted down as a sacrifice to Hitler in the second world war.

Perhaps one of the fishermen would lead the service, or there might be a visiting evangelist, or even a Salvation Army group, but, whoever the preacher might be, the threat of hell fire and the hope of salvation resounded along Cromwell Street.

As the pubs disgorged at closing time (when there were pubs in Stornoway — and that's another story!) and the derelicts which you find in any seaport town came staggering along, they were swallowed up in a crowd of scores of squat, broad shouldered, leather skinned Buchan fishermen, transported more completely from the hardships of their earthly lot than the drunks themselves, and, in the excitement of their revivalist hymns, almost as intoxicated.

Sometimes, through the columns of the People's Journal one could watch the progress of a revival round the coast from fishing port to fishing port until finally it reached ourselves.

On Sunday most of the Buchan fishermen went to Martin's Memorial. It had not then been named in honour of its first minister but was officially the U.F. (English) congregation, or popularly the Free English, because it was the only Presbyterian Church in town in which Gaelic was never used.

The church hall was set aside on Saturdays as a writing-room for the fishermen. So far as I know no other provision was made locally at that time for the great seasonal influx of visiting fishermen.

On Sunday evening, an hour before the service was due to start, the church was opened with the organist in attendance, to lead the fishermen in a programme of Moody and Sankey revivalist hymns.

By the time the ordinary congregation arrived the church was full, or more than full. At times chairs had to be set in the aisles for the latecomers.

No one who has ever heard it can forget the sound of three or four hundred Buchan fishermen singing with all the strength of their lungs, and the passion of their hearts, and the beauty of their rich melodious voices, "Will your anchor hold in the storms of life?", or "Hear us when we cry to Thee for those in peril on the sea." Or triumphantly, "Ye gates lift up your heads on high."

A few hundred yards along the street one could hear another sound, more elemental, seemingly less disciplined. Rising and falling like the sea itself, in apparent confusion, but still with a deep controlling rhythm. Throwing off grace notes in great profusion like the iridescent spray from a breaking wave. Carrying the same message aloft to the same God in an older and even more intoxicating tongue.

I was in the midst of the Moody and Sankey revivalist hymns, because we attended the Free English. I heard the Gaelic Psalms and Paraphrases from the Free Church as an eavesdropper. Standing outside the wall, often alone, immovable, in the dark. Comforted by the glow from the church windows. Unable to understand the words, but carried away by the strange primeval quality of the music.

When I was a little bit older, and we had moved house from Lewis Street to Matheson Road, I listened more frequently to the singing in the Free Prsbyterian Church. Again, standing in the dark, pondering on the mystery of it all.

It was that contrast between the singing in our own church, and the singing in the others, perhaps more than anything else, that made me first aware, in a vague way, that I lived, not only on an island, but in an island within an island.

A small, middle class, English speaking, urban and cosmopolitan community, in a constant state of flux, as new arrivals or departures changed the balance of accents, temperaments and skills, enclosed by more than seven times its number of Gaelic-speaking crofter fishermen, living in a hundred scattered villages which had endured over the centuries, changing — until then — almost as imperceptibly as the grey unyielding gneiss on which they stood.

It was only on latha na drobh, the day of the annual cattle market, that the other Lewis, the real Lewis, invaded and possessed the town.

Although the Gaelic singing in the churches was quite foreign to me, and the majority of the Lewis fishermen on the boats in Stornoway harbour used, for preference, a language which I did not understand, they were all somehow part of the town.

But, on market day, I became aware of the existence of rural Lewis, the exclusively Gaelic-speaking community, of which the Gaelic intrusions into the town, as they appeared to be, were merely the outliers.

The relationship between Stornoway and Lewis has always been complex.

The burgh is at the same time the most Gaelic town in Scotland and the most Anglicised part of the Outer Hebrides, and it has been so for generations, indeed for centuries.

There is an inevitable tension between town and country — the interface between two cultures. It is probably less now than it has ever been, thanks to the motor car, and the "Comhairle" — a phenomenon I will refer to later.

When I was a youngster the town children spoke of the country children as Maoris, although I have no recollection of ever having heard the phrase used in the home. Indeed I have a suspicion that it was probably more used by families in the process of transition from country to town than by those who were urban by birth.

Be that as it may, my friend the Breve squared the account when he defined a Stornowegian as anyone born between "Tigh nan Guts in Inacleit and the Ocrach in Ceann a Bhaigh," — "The Gut House in Inaclete and the midden in Bayhead." Even for an English speaker like me it sounds better in Gaelic.

Tigh nan Guts is still with us, but the Ocrach has disappeared. Nothing remains in the memory but the acrid smell of burning refuse. But the Breve's definition is an apt one and puts SY's in their place.

And yet, if a Lewisman travelling away from home is asked where he comes from, he will almost certainly say "Stornoway", whether he comes in fact from the town; from the villages immediately adjacent, like Laxdale and Sandwick; from Brenish, forty five miles away perched high on the cliffs above the Atlantic, looking westward to Labrador; or even from Tobson or Kirkibost, in a different island altogether, which swaggers across the map as Great Bernera, a name which seems to diminish the larger island lying alongside, and the port of which it is so proud.

Why should this be?

It is a mystery worth a little probing, even if there are no certain answers.

10
Gaelic has a word for it

Moray McLaren in his entry on Stornoway in the Shell Guide to Scotland says it is the "only example of a town purely Gaelic in its making and not one imposed by incomers."

That is a very perceptive comment, which I have not seen made elsewhere. It needs to be said. But it also needs some modification.

Incomers have not made Stornoway but they have made a considerable contribution to it. It would have been a poorer town without them.

And many of the Gaelic-speaking business men who contributed largely to the town's development were trying to divest themselves of Gaelic, rather than to cherish it. That is part of our problem. At times we confused the baby with the bath water.

It is significant that when Donald Morrison, the Harris cooper, sat down in Stornoway, in the early years of last century, with a board across his knees for a desk, to record the ancient traditions of his native island he wrote in English.

I have been shocked at times myself to hear Stornowegians boast that the town has a Woolworths, as if being the same as every other town in Britain was a mark of distinction, rather than having a language and culture of one's own.

Lewis was passing an important watershed at the time of which I am writing. The boys and girls who were growing up in rural Lewis when I was a boy in Stornoway, were the last generation of Lewis children who had no English when they went to school.

The line of demarcation between Gaelic and English was sharper than it is today, and, although there was a great deal of Gaelic spoken in Stornoway, the frontier of language and the frontier between town and country were roughly the same. Or appeared to be roughly the same because the true situation was masked.

The great fleet of S.Y's was largely owned, and almost wholly manned, by Gaelic-speakers from the rural villages. The fishergirls were also mostly Gaelic-speakers from the rural villages. But to me, as a growing boy, both fishermen and fishergirls were part of the Stornoway scene. My contact with them was purely visual. I was hardly conscious of their speech.

I was fully aware of their presence in town, but did not see the significance of their absence when they vanished at weekends into the surrounding countryside.

On latha na drobh the country folk came to town, but not as fishermen returning to resume their week's work in the vessels which had lain in the harbour even in their absence. They came as crofters, driving flocks of sheep, or herds of cattle. Or riding in little red and blue carts, or brown varnished pony traps. Or leading shaggy horses to the sale ring.

They came from a world that was quite unlike my own, even although at that time

28

many Stornoway families kept a cow or two, as my grannie did, and cultivated an allotment at the back of the town.

And they came in such numbers that Cromwell Street looked as if it might burst apart with the pressure of slow-moving humanity, in the evening, when the market was over and the day's earnings were being liberally spent in the pubs, and we youngsters were reluctant to go to bed, lingering on the streets late into the night in the hope of seeing a fight, which we very often did.

I suppose the girls from the country districts came to the market too, but if they did I have no recollection of them.

It is the boys who march vividly before me as I write. Tall gangling youths with a lumbering athleticism in their gait. The product not of organised games or work in a gymnasium, but of tramping broken moorland, scrambling on cliffs, and jumping in and out of restless boats launched from rocky geos or open beaches.

All of them wore caps. Huge cloth caps that seemed many times too big for them. Their floppy brims were generally supported by a willow withy frame so that they stood out like sunhats or sombreros without a crown.

And corduroy knickerbockers unfastened at the knee so that they hung half way down the leg, looking as inadequate and untidy as the caps were excessive but kempt.

Many of them carried walking sticks, or if they didn't, the purchase of one was the first priority when they got to the fairground, with its stalls and its circus, and its coconut shies.

I can hear as I write the lowing of cattle, the baaing of sheep, and neighing of horses. I can feel myself slithering on the sodden, muddy, churned up turf, for it was almost always raining. I can see Sime's toy stall. Taste Finlay's ice cream.

May and June are the loveliest months of the year in Lewis — apart from September. The twilight lingers so that there is almost no night and a steady east wind brings long spells of bracing sunshine. It seemed stupid, almost to the point of perversity, to hold the annual cattle market, one of the great social and commercial occasions of the year, in the month of July when the sultry rain storms were so predictable that they came to be known as "tuiltean na drobh," — "the market downpours".

For us town children, who could not show, by sporting a staff or a shepherd's crook, that we had come to man's estate, and were used to handling sheep at the fank or on the moor, the great prizes of the market, apart from a visit to the circus, were the coconuts and "aran cridhe".

How is it possible to make the affluent Lewis child of today understand a world in which a piece of gingerbread was an unusual and sought-for treat? Or that a dance at the road end, under a canopy of stars, with a solitary melodeon for accompaniment, or no instrumental music at all, can give more undiluted enjoyment than evenings spent in a sophisticated dance hall with a famous band, an open bar, and all the money you can spend?

The greatest pleasures come at the margins of what we have, and we were fortunate that our margins were low. Our desires easily satisfied.

My own first market was a day of dismal rain, but I dragged my mother with me, determined to sample a coconut, that ambrosial delight, that mysterious and legendary fruit of which I had heard so much but which I had never tasted or even seen.

29

I can still feel the urgency as we ploughed through the mud together past Willowglen house, and along to the Stile Park, where the market was held at that time. And the fury of frustration which choked me when we had to leave the road and stand in the rain on the grassy bank to let a cart or a gig or a cow go by. Every pause seemed like an eternity.

As soon as I acquired my coconut I was impatient to be home again to eat it. The rest of the market meant nothing to me, I had achieved my goal. The great goal of my life, as it seemed.

When I got back to Lewis Street I bashed the coconut against the coal shed wall with all my might but no result. There was no way in which I could break into the mysterious, delightful interior.

Finally my father, or perhaps my brother, came to my assistance, and I had my first taste of coconut.

How often have I thought of that incident since when something I have striven for has turned to dust and ashes in my mouth?

There is no word I know of in the English language which adequately describes the disappointment, the chagrin, the disillusionment, of that first bite.

But Gaelic has one!

Tamailt!

11
The Night The Roof Blew Off

I was already familiar with the word tamailt when I had my disappointment with the coconut, but I did not know it was Gaelic!

It was much later I came to realise that Gaelic often has a word for a human experience, less precise but more sharply descriptive than English.

Paradoxically the lack of precision may be part of the explanation of the sharpness. It invites us to apply our minds and imaginations to the situation. To interpret it in the light of all the surrounding circumstances.

Lack of precision also leaves scope for little nuances of emphasis or expression. Words which are narrowly and sharply defined make prisoners of our thought just as surely as they give clarity to it.

It is the sort of difference which makes the violin a more expressive, if more limited, instrument than the piano.

As a child I was quite unaware of the fact that many of the words I needed to express myself were borrowed from another tongue. Even yet I am often surprised when my wife teases me for using Gaelic idioms in English.

Knowing both languages, Cathie can keep them apart in her mind. Knowing only the one, I have more difficulty in purging myself of intrusive colloquialisms.

It is part of the paradox of Lewis, and one that often makes me feel ashamed, that Cathie who was born in Hartford, Connecticut, speaks Gaelic fluently, while I, who was born in Stornoway, do not.

Both Cathie's parents were Gaelic-speakers, but it was only when the family returned to Lewis that she learned the language.

She was ten at the time, and suddenly found herself transported from a large modern American school where discipline was free and easy, to a small, strict, old-fashioned village school in Lewis where the children spoke Gaelic in the playground, and her clothes, accent and mannerisms all marked her out as a stranger, until she acquired the defensive camouflage of language and disappeared into the landscape like her playmates.

On their first day in Tong school her younger sister, Anna, shattered the disciplined calm of the classroom by announcing, as she might have done in the American school with which they were familiar, "I guess I'll go next door and see my sister, Sheila".

When the startled teacher had recovered sufficently to expostulate, Anna calmly replied, "That ain't going to hurt anyone", and strode from the room.

It didn't happen a second time. The old Lewis had a way of reasserting itself over those who came back, but it was important in the life of the community that there was this process of emigration and return, sustained over a very long period of time.

A little earlier than the time I am writing of we find Stornoway with a provost, (chief magistrate I think he was called then,) known to everyone as "California", for the most obvious of reasons. Go back a hundred years from that and you find a Stornoway business man being asked to interpret in a court case because he had learned French in Upper Canada.

Moray McLaren in the comment on Stornoway I have already quoted made the point that the town was purely Gaelic in its making, and not imposed by incomers. He should have added, however, to be strictly truthful, that many of the Gaelic-speaking natives were themselves "incomers" in a very real sense. Returned natives bringing with them more than a whiff of the outside world.

Stornoway developed because it was not a closed community, and the local attitude to Gaelic was always complex and always changing.

My schooldays coincided with slack water in the Gaelic renaissance, if renaissance, as I hope, it proves to be.

The centuries of repression were over. It was no longer the official policy to "extirpate" the native tongue. But, at the same time, little constructive was being done in the schools to save it. Or even to use it in circumstances where its use, by any standard, made educational sense.

My maternal grandmother was a fluent Gaelic speaker, and took a pride in the language, but her family seem to have had a rather equivocal attitude to it.

Roddie, her eldest son, preached in Gaelic and English with equal facility. His English sermons were logical and diamond sharp, not a word wasted, no overtones of sentiment or emotionalism. His Gaelic sermons were also esteemed, but I can hardly imagine that he used the same spare style. I may be wrong, but I feel that a Gaelic sermon could not have been so closely contained.

Willie, who was only a few years younger had little Gaelic when he left Stornoway to go to university. He acquired the language when he was serving his apprenticeship in a local chemist's shop. He became the Gaelic enthusiast in the family, although, (perhaps because!) his working life was spent as a doctor in a mining village in Durham.

He translated "Julius Caesar" and "Rip Van Winkle" into Gaelic and invented for his own amusement a Gaelic shorthand.

His Gaelic, though fluent enough, was, I am told, too literary, and once when he delivered an eloquent Gaelic oration at a Mod concert in Stornoway, one of his cousins — who, as far as I know, had no Gaelic at all — told him, rather snidely, that he spoke like the tinkers.

The younger members of the family had less Gaelic than the older, and my mother was youngest of all.

She was still a babe in arms when the old thatched house, which stood on the same site as the house I knew as "grannie's" was destroyed, in the winter of 1877.

Nearly eighty years after the event, Bella, the oldest of my aunts, told me the story.

There had been a week of exceptionally violent gales. They began on a Sunday night. Bella heard a great commotion outside the house. As she peered into the darkness she saw Aeneas Mackenzie, one of the leading ship owners in the town, hurrying by, shouting "Gilsland ahoy! Gilsland ahoy!" as a helpless vessel was driven on the beach, almost on to my grannie's doorstep. There was no wall then, and the sea lapped up to the Newton doors.

In the morning the Gilsland was gone. Smashed by the gale. But her cargo of

32

wheat was spread along the shore. The Newton folk gathered it in buckets and took it to the mill where it was ground into wheaten meal.

The mill was at the Manor Farm where the Caberfeidh hotel is now, and I well remember the great mill wheel and the lade, which were among the wonders of my boyhood.

Night after night, Bella told me, the wind battered the house. On the following Sunday night she and Roddie and my granny were still up at midnight, afraid to go to bed, the storm was so violent.

Suddenly Bella screamed. She had looked up and saw the sky. The roof had been carried away. The younger children were wakened, but the family stayed in the roofless house all night, Roddie holding my mother in his arms.

In the morning they went to their aunt's home a few doors along the street where they got shelter for a year and a half until my grandfather returned from the voyage he was on, and built the present house. The aunt was Mrs Smith, great grandmother of Sandy Matheson now Convener of the Comhairle.

It was typical of my Spartan, self-reliant grandmother that she spent the night in a roofless house rather than disturb her sister.

My mother had only a smattering of Gaelic, and would not trust herself to use it. When the fish wives from Broad Bay came round the door with their creels calling "An Ceannaich sibh iasg!", they conversed quite happily, the one in Gaelic and the other in English, each understanding what the other said, but unwilling to risk exposure in the less familiar tongue.

12
Don't Do It Again!

Some of the youngsters with whom I first went to school in Stornoway must have been Gaelic speakers. But it was not spoken in the playground or the classroom.

Indeed many of my early classmates were from the south of England, because Stornoway was an important naval base. My immediate friends had names like Stanley and Partridge rather than Macleod.

Others were members of East Coast families which had come to Stornoway because of the fishing. I can still recall my astonishment when one of my particular friends, Thomson Bruce, broke off a discussion we were having in Stornoway slang, to speak to his mother in the broadest Buchan.

I knew by that time that Gaelic and English were different languages, but it was a great surprise to discover that there were two different kinds of English, one of which was incomprehensible.

I doubt if at that time many of my teachers were fluent Gaelic speakers either. For the most part they were drawn from my own relatively narrow family circle.

The seven teachers I had in the primary and elementary school were all natives of Stornoway. Two lived within a hundred yards of my home. A third was my cousin. A fourth was married to a cousin, and still another was connected with my mother's family by marriage.

School was just an extension of the family. I was allowed no special liberties, but I was among friends whose outlook and attitude was very close to that of my parents.

One of the seven, in fact one of the two who lived quite close to us, did speak Gaelic — Chrissie Macarthur — and it was through her I had my first direct contact with the language.

She tried to teach me to sing "Tha mi sgith" and other Gaelic songs, but the attempt was short lived. Chrissie had a brusque but kindly manner. One day, during the music lesson, she glowered round the class, and demanded, "Who's the boy who's singing in his boots?". She quickly identified the culprit, and I was banished to do sums in the cloakroom.

I never sang in a school choir again until timid little Miss Garioch drafted me back in, during my last year in school, to help her maintain discipline, but with strict instructions to keep my mouth shut.

I didn't hold it against Chrissie Macarthur that she expelled me from the music class, because she had other unconventional but endearing ways.

Every Friday she set us five sums, and as soon as we were finished we were permitted to read our favourite comic. On condition that we provided one for her as well!

Being reasonably good at sums I had a pleasant Friday most weeks in her class, even although I, and the other early finishers, had to sit on the hot water pipes at the back of the room, so that we could drop quickly out of sight if any unexpected visitor should arrive — as the Rector, Mr Gibson, did on at least one occasion.

The chance to read "Chums" in class while the teacher read "The Boys Cinema" more than made up for the indignity of not being allowed to sing songs, which in any event I did not understand, and had some difficulty in pronouncing.

In the secondary department of the school it was different. The majority of the pupils came from the rural districts. Indeed for several years I was the only boy on the class who was not a native Gaelic speaker.

At that stage it was easier to divest myself of the little knowledge that I did have, and pretend that I had none, than expose myself to ridicule by speaking Gaelic haltingly to those who had it as their mother tongue.

It is a natural human reaction to despise what we do not possess, or at any rate affect to despise it.

It was this sort of pride, this unwillingness to accept that what we do not understand has any value, the reluctance of educated people to admit that crofters and fishermen commanded two languages when they had only one, which explains (in part at least) the quite deplorable attitude of Scottish educationists to Gaelic down almost to the present day.

It was reinforced by fear. The Lowlander's fear of the unruly Highlander, which was a very real consideration well into the 19th century, and also by a grossly materialistic attitude to education.

But, for much the same reasons, many of the educationists who sought to eradicate Gaelic in the Highlands were, at the same time, divesting themselves of their native Scots, and many Gaelic-speaking teachers approved without question the anti-Gaelic policies they were asked to pursue.

Attitudes to language are much more complex than they are generally represented to be, and many of those who are strongly pro-Gaelic today might well have been on the other side of the argument if they had been born half a century earlier.

In my father's time as a reporter it was not unusual for a trial in the Sheriff Court to be conducted wholly in Gaelic because the accused had no English. That never happened in mine, but it was still occasionally necessary to have a Gaelic interpreter for an elderly witness. Indeed a Gaelic interpreter was used in one of the last cases I reported, in the middle fifties.

The witness concerned referred several times to a house the family were supposed to be building. The Sheriff had some doubt whether the house really existed. "Put it to her that this was just a castle in the air," he said to the interpreter.

The question was put and the witness replied. The interpreter then turned to the Sheriff and said, "No my lord. In Lower Bayble!"

The interpreter in my father's time was George the Gaoler, an ex-policeman with a mind of his own. On one occasion, when the Sheriff returned a "not proven" verdict, and explained at length why he could not find the accused guilty, George succinctly interpreted the decision into Gaelic as "His Lordship says you can go this time but don't do it again."

In one of the first cases I reported myself, a witness asked for the services of an interpreter. The bar officer, known to us all affectionately as Jacko, was sworn in for the purpose.

His understanding of Gaelic was no doubt adequate but he relied heavily on English words which he Gaelicised. At one point the witness, who had professed to

35

have no English, questioned the accuracy of Jacko's interpretation of his answer, and did so in perfect English.

Sheriff MacInnes, an able but consequential little man, gave the witness a dressing-down for having misled the Court, and withdrew the services of the interpreter.

I reported the incident in the daily press. An Comunn Gaidhealach protested at the Sheriff's remarks. Eventually questions were asked in Parliament.

One evening the Sheriff asked me to see him in his room in the Royal Hotel. He showed me a letter he had just received from the Scottish Office asking him to report on the incident. He suggested quite blatantly that I should write the Secretary of State and say the press reports had been inaccurate.

It was a difficult situation. I was not only an inexperienced reporter working entirely on my own, with no one to corroborate my report, I was also one of the Sheriff's own officials, being shorthand writer to the Court.

I told him I was not prepared to disown the report because it was completely accurate, but I was prepared to write the Secretary of State and say that the witness had given him some provocation.

MacInnes was very displeased, but, so far as I can recall, he bore no grudge.

13
The Supreme Penalty for Bigamy

After his brush with An Comunn and Parliament, Sheriff MacInnes was much more discreet in his approach to Gaelic. He made no fuss over taking evidence in Gaelic from two old ladies who were the chief witnesses in a separation case which arose a little later — the only matrimonial dispute I had to report in more than thirty years regular attendance at the Sheriff Court.

The old ladies were the mothers of the two spouses. Neither could come to court, and their evidence had to be taken in their own homes. We visited the first in an attic in Bayhead, the second in a house in Lochs. They gave very different versions of the dispute.

According to the husband's mother the trouble was caused exclusively by the wife. According to the wife's mother it was caused exclusively by the husband.

As we came out of the second house Sheriff MacInnes said to Charlie Anderson, the Sheriff Clerk, "Have you ever heard the story of Tim Healy, the famous Irish Q.C.?"

"No," said Charlie.

"He was appearing in a matrimonial dispute," said the Sheriff, "and made repeated references to 'the supreme penalty for bigamy'. At last one of the judges interposed, 'But what is the supreme penalty for bigamy?'. 'To have two mothers-in-law', replied Mr Healy."

Although MacInnes made no demur when the witnesses asked to be examined in Gaelic there was a little contretemps in the house in Lochs.

The Sheriff asked a question. It was translated and the witness made a lengthy reply. Jacko, acting as interpreter, gave the answer in one word, 'No!'

Another question followed with another long reply from the witness which Jacko translated succinctly as 'Yes!'

"That's not good enough," said the Sheriff, "I want to know the whole answer."

Jacko patiently explained that the old lady had hurt herself by bumping into a half-opened door, and before replying to each question, she apologised at length to his Lordship for her black eye. Exercising a sensible discretion he had omitted the apologies from the replies.

In the very last case I reported — many years later, long after Sheriff MacInnes was dead — one of the witnesses had a language problem. Even with the oath.

"I swear by Almighty God. I swear where I am going," she said.

"What's she saying?" demanded Sheriff Miller. "I know where I'm going?"

Colin Scott Mackenzie, the Fiscal, suggested that the witness would be more at ease in Gaelic.

"Do you know any English?" asked the Sheriff.

"No," said the witness. In English.

The Sheriff, however, consented to let her give her evidence in Gaelic in which she was obviously happier.

The interpreter was still Jacko, hale and hearty in his seventies, ready on the slightest excuse, to dance a jig with the step of a sixteen year old, on the stone flags at the entrance to the Court House as we waited for a case to begin.

I believe he might even have been tempted at times to show that he could still do a hand-stand as he did once, many years before, as a bit of sex display when he was courting.

His rival was as tall as Jacko was short. By some mischance they arrived at the lady's house together. One of the old houses up a stair in a close off Cromwell Street, now absorbed into Murdo Maclean's furniture store, if I mistake not.

The rooms were low, and, as they waited there uncomfortably for the lady to appear and sort things out, the tall suitor stood up and placed the palm of his hand flat against the ceiling.

"Can you do that?" he said to Jacko with a sneer.

"No!" said Jacko, "but can you do that?"

As he spoke, he kicked his boots off, turned a somersault on to the table, and placed his stockinged soles against the ceiling.

I don't know whether that was the decisive moment in Jacko's love affair, nor even whether the lady concerned was the one he ultimately married, but he was still chuckling over his rival's discomfiture when he told me the story more than half a century after it happened.

Remembering my experiences in the Stornoway Sheriff Court I was always ready in the Crofters Commission to use Gaelic where that appeared to be an advantage. By law, at least one of the Commissioners must be a Gaelic speaker and in the early years the Commission also had a Gaelic-speaking Secretary — Donald MacCuish who has done so much since his retirement for An Comunn Gaidhealach — and a Gaelic-speaking Chief Technical Officer — the late Alex Macarthur, who was for many years a member of the Glasgow Islay Choir.

In honesty it must be said, however, that, even when we had important issues explained in Gaelic, Gaelic was never used in the subsequent discussion by the crofters themselves, but only by schoolteachers and other professional people who could clearly have used English just as well.

In my eighteen years with the Commission I was only once asked to have a hearing conducted in Gaelic. That was in Uist, and the request came from a schoolmaster who was violently opposed to the course of action the Commission, at the request of some of the crofters, proposed to pursue.

I had a feeling that he made the request only to embarrass me, because there was no one in the Commission party on that occasion who could speak Gaelic. I resolved the difficulty by acceding to the request — and inviting the Schoolmaster himself to be the interpreter.

Even when Gaelic was not used as a medium of communication I sometimes tried to enliven an informal but stodgy meeting by asking for a Gaelic song.

One of the great problems in a body like the Crofters Commission is to know, at an early stage, whether the parties to a dispute are completely irreconcilable, so that one must stand aloof and conduct the hearing with great formality, like a court, and give a ruling, or whether, by working informally from within the situation, there is a chance of effecting a settlement.

38

In the latter situation a good poaching story or a Gaelic song can be a marvellous solvent of suspicion. But there are times when the only effective weapon is the bludgeon.

Once when Norman Buchan was touring the Islands as Under Secretary of State for Scotland we had a rather heavy meeting with the Commission Assessors in Lochboisdale Hotel.

At the end of it, knowing Norman Buchan's interest in folk music, I suggested that John Macinnes, the District Clerk and one of our Assessors, should give us a song.

John gave us "Kishmul's Galley" in Gaelic as he had heard it sung in Barra by a traditional singer, and then in English as it has been tarted up by Mrs Kennedy Fraser.

It was a tremendous performance with just a hint of satire to give it a bite.

The Under Secretary insisted on having it all a second time.

We probably achieved more in that ten minutes of song than in the whole of the discussion which preceeded it.

14
Which Came First — Back or Point?

Around the time of my meeting in Uist with Norman Buchan, or perhaps a little later, I had a discussion about Gaelic over breakfast in the Invershin Hotel with two members of the Commission staff.

Ann Macleod who belonged to Uig said she had two words of English when she went to school. "Yes" and "No". She knew that one was affirmative and the other negative, but she did not know which was which.

She gave us a very amusing account of a conversation she had with a visitor to Uig who had no Gaelic. She used her two words of English alternately in the hope that he would not notice that she had no idea what he was saying.

Suddenly she realised, by the look on his face, that she had used the wrong word in some disastrous context.

"If you had two words of English going to school", commented Donald MacCuish, "you were better equipped than I was. I had none."

They both agreed that they had found no difficulty going straight into a foreign language when their schooling began. They were anxious to learn and accepted that that was the only way they could.

It must have been very different, however, for those whose intelligence and ambition to succeed was insufficient to take them easily over the language threshold.

Whatever the effect on the children, the educational approach to Gaelic made complete nonsense of the general method of language teaching them in vogue.

Latin and French were taught laboriously, by grammar and syntax from the printed page, and, not suprisingly, children were thought to be incapable of attempting so difficult a discipline until they were into their teens.

I find it difficult to understand how this approach to language could have been persisted in by an Education Department which thought it not incongruous to teach Gaelic-speaking children reading, writing and arithmetic, and the abstruse, pedantic irrelevancies of the shorter catechism in English at the age of five.

The old attitude to Gaelic was not only stupid, it was cruel, and, at times there was an element of sadism. How dared the little blighters know a language that their masters didn't!

But that is not terribly relevant to the position of Gaelic at the present day, and considerable damage can be done by importing into the current situation a sense of grievance from the past.

When the crofters were campaigning, in the eighties of last century, for security in their holdings, they were also campaigning for Gaelic-speaking teachers and inspectors in the schools.

Educationalists have now, largely, come round to the view that the crofters were right, but, in the meantime, many Gaelic-speaking parents and Gaelic-speaking teachers have become so indoctrinated with the educational heresies in which they were brought up there is some doubt whether the will to preserve the language still exists on a wide enough base.

This is not to argue that the attempt should not be made. It should. It is merely to suggest that the task is more complex and difficult than is sometimes realised.

There is a job of persuasion, perhaps even conversion, to be carried out in the Gaelic heartland itself which is more urgent and more important than the persuasion of Parliament.

There are encouraging signs, but the situation is manifestly very different from the situation which existed when Donald MacCuish, Ann Macleod and I were at school, within the same island, two of us coming from a home environment that was wholly Gaelic, the third from a home environment that was exclusively English.

At this point in time it is difficult for me to be sure whether my own first direct contact with rural Lewis — Gaelic Lewis — was at the old schoolhouse in Back on the north side of Broad Bay, or in the village of Knock on the south side where Anna Pope was married and had a croft.

Anna was my second cousin, but she was older than my mother, or so she appeared to me. I always thought of her as Stephen MacLean's aunt rather than any relative of my own.

It was her brother Willie who figured in the episode of the tarred bottoms, and she had the same rollicking sense of fun, as had all the Popes, except perhaps Jessie, who never married, and was one of the grand ladies of the town, of which there were quite a few in those days.

As a child I was often puzzled to understand how so elegant and proper a lady as Jessie Pope could be the sister of a plain, homely shop assistant's wife, who lived on her husband's croft, kept a cow and hens, cut peats and went to the airidh. But there was no doubt which of them I preferred to visit.

Stephen and I occasionally cycled to Knock, and that was quite an adventure for several reasons. The waterbound roads were rougher than a shingle beach, but when we saw one of the little carts from Point we got our heads low over the handlebars and pedalled as fast as we could, however rough the going.

Feeling between town and country was high and some of the Point youngsters had a habit of slashing at us with the whip as we went by. I have no recollection of ever being actually hit, and I have a suspicion that they were more anxious to see us cowering than to do us harm.

Although it is difficult to know why they resented boys on bicycles it was natural that there should be ill-feeling between carters and motorists (or motor cyclists). On a narrow road a noisy car was an uncomfortable neighbour for a restive horse.

I have often seen my father grit his teeth and exercise extreme patience, when a carter quite deliberately took the crown of the road and prevented our motor cycle from passing for as long as he possibly could.

It was said that old Macdougal, who had a cycle agent's shop at the corner of Church Street and Kenneth Street, and who was one of the first in the island to have a motor cycle, once took the silencer off to clear the highway by scaring all the horses for miles around.

It is probably apocryphal, but the story went that one particularly stubborn carter was last seen, on that occasion, heading for the Golf Course and the sea at breakneck speed, his horse completely out of control.

41

My visits to Back were less frequent than my visits to Knock, but longer. The schoolmaster's wife was my mother's best friend, and I was roughly co-ages with their son Ian. When my mother went down for a few days' stay, I went with her.

Ian's father was a good schoolmaster in the old tradition. A strict disciplinarian, and a sound classical scholar. Rather unusually for a Lewis headmaster of that generation he had a wide knowledge of music.

He served the community well, both within the school and outside it, but he did not belong to it, despite the fact that his name was Morrison. He was an alien intruder in a Gaelic village, as I would have been myself.

Ian, not unnaturally, tried to identify himself with the children he was brought up amongst. He was almost aggressive in his attachment to Gaelic. He despised classical music but learned the bagpipes. And he was determined to go to sea like all the boys around him.

15
The House that went to Sea

On one occasion some of us were twitting Ian Morrison on his partiality for the bagpipes. We were fond of the pipes ourselves, and would follow the pipe band endlessly through the streets when it was on parade, but, at the time, it seemed as good a stick as any to beat him with in friendly banter.

"Who ever heard of bagpipes in an orchestra?" asked one of the group.

"Who ever heard of a piano at the head of an army?" came Ian's reply.

At that point the teasing abruptly ended.

Ian's parents wished him to go to university, as he could well have done. But he had other ideas. He worked hard — and it really did require an effort from a really bright lad — to fail his exams, convincingly.

I can still recall his whoop of triumph when the results of the Quarterlies were posted up, and Ian was last on the class.

He came bouncing through the door of Springfield School — the Tech. as we called it, and there is a bit of educational history in the name — shouting to all and sundry, with unrestrained glee, "Tha mi fhin thirty-third! Tha mi fhin thirty-third!"

At that stage his parents saw the wisdom of letting him have his way.

When he left for the training ship *"Conway"*, I gave him a fountain pen as a hint that I would like to keep in touch, but he was no correspondent, nor for that matter was I. When last I heard of him he was sailing on the Queensland coast, but that was many years ago.

In my youth, however, he was the person who brought me closest to the real Lewis.

Back Schoolhouse, like most of the other Lewis schools and school houses, stood well apart from the villages it served. Placed in no man's land, so to speak, to be equidistant from as many centres of population as possible. In this way our thrifty ancestors made one school do the work of two or three. At a price!

The children from Coll and Vatisker had long distances to walk along exposed roads, often lashed by wind and rain. There were no school buses, and no school canteens.

In spite of their addiction to the classics the authorities had clearly forgotten the well known Latin tag about sound minds in sound bodies.

The result as we shall see later, was a virulent "epidemic" of tuberculosis in which I lost several of my closest friends.

Back Schoolhouse was not entirely isolated although it was well clear of the village. The Police Station was nearby, and we were occasionally entertained by stories of one policeman's wife whose English was a little "seldom" — the phrase we used in mockery.

Once she confided that her husband was off work because he had a "swallow in his eye."

It never occurred to me that the policeman's wife was much more proficient in my language than I was in hers. Tolerance and understanding are not natural human attributes. They are disciplines slowly acquired through living in a civilised and ordered society — and very often not acquired at all.

Also near the schoolhouse was a little corrugated iron mission house of the Church of Scotland, where we used to worship on Sunday. I cannot recall the appearance of the interior, nor anything that I heard there. My one recollection is of my amusement and delight, as a sophisticated townee, to discover that the collection was taken in an ordinary soup plate, borrowed for the purpose from someone's kitchen.

The congregation was tiny. Most of the villagers belonged to the Free Church, as they still do. It was a much larger building, standing prominently on the skyline, so that in those days, when there were few navigational aids, it served fishermen miles away in the Minch as a bearing point. I have heard it used in that way to fix the position of a poaching trawler in the Sheriff Court.

On Sunday morning in Back I realised much more clearly than in Stornoway, that I belonged to a cultural enclave, using a different language, and worshipping in a different church, from the great majority, but still so parochial in my outlook, so convinced of my own superiority, that I felt no need to merge myself in the majority as Ian had done, and smugly laughed at the solecisms of the policeman's Gaelic-speaking wife.

Looking out from the schoolhouse I could see below me, across a little burn, the thatched houses of Vatisker. When I visit Vatisker nowadays, to call on my brother-in-law, and see the sturdy modern houses, I marvel that Lewis can be so completely different, and yet so completely the same.

The transformation could not have been achieved without state aid. The crofters have had substantial grants and loans for housing for many years, although they were, and still are much less heavily subsidised than many tenants of Council houses in the cities of the south, who think they are carrying the crofters on their backs.

It took a lot of argument, when I first raised the issue, to get St Andrew's House to produce comparative figures, and, even after they had been produced, it took some time for their significance to sink in.

Even with state aid, the transformation could not have been achieved without great efforts by the crofters themselves. The prospective tenant of a council house has nothing to do but put his name on the list and wait. Or pull a few strings, if he has the opportunity. But the crofter, at every stage, must take the initiative himself.

The efforts the crofters made to improve their homes was perhaps best illustrated by the half-houses of Tolsta which were a familiar sight between the wars.

They were tiny cottages solidly built on three sides, but with one gable roughly boarded up, waiting for the day the family could afford to pull the boarding down and build the other half of the house.

They looked odd, mis-shapen, truncated buildings, in their half-finished form, but how they gave the lie to the myth that the islander is lazy and shiftless and lacking in enterprise.

The east coast crofter and the Orcadian tend to put their major effort into building their steadings. The home comes second. With the west coaster, the home comes first. This may reflect a genuine difference in temperament and social values.

On the other hand it may be that each has adjusted to his environment. The land in the east is worth investing in, but there is a limit to the amount of capital the tiny crofts in the west can sustain.

At the end of the second world war, when building materials were unobtainable, one or two Lewis families built themselves little wooden shacks to live in, set on a much larger concrete foundation.

When money and materials became available they built a permanent dwelling around the shack on the foundations already laid. When it was ready, they dismantled the shack and used the timber for flooring.

One man, completely stuck for building materials, bought a derelict house in Glen Tolsta. He could not get in with wheeled transport to take out the timber he wanted to reclaim, because, at that time, there was no road. But the house was near the shore, so he built a raft with the timber, and, well equipped with food and verey lights, sailed out into Broad Bay, and so to a beach accessible to lorries.

My personal knowledge of Lewis goes back for nearly three quarters of a century. Through my father's scrapbook, and my uncle's reminiscences, and my own study of social history, I have known the people, in a sense, for over a hundred years. Always as a detached observer.

I have seen them lift themselves by the bootstraps out of abject poverty. They are adaptable, ingenious, hard-working, not easily dismayed or turned aside from their purpose, although at times they were bemused by the odd mixture of neglect, stupidity and misplaced paternalism with which so many governments treated them.

My faith in their readiness to respond to opportunity is never higher than when I am approaching Vatisker, past the old Back school, and think of the huddle of thatched houses I knew there as a child.

16
Teeth of the Affluent

We spent a lot of time — Ian Morrison and I — scrambling over the rocks, or down on the beach at Brevig watching the boats come in.

I was fascinated by the ritual of dividing up the catch and drawing lots for the various heaps. And I was aware even then, probably Ian told me, that there was always one share set aside for widows and others who had no one to provide for them.

And always there was something for the stranger lad from the town who stood tongue-tied on the fringe of the Gaelic-speaking crowd. One of the great moments of my life was when one of the skippers gave me a huge skate to carry back to the schoolhouse on my finger, like a man.

A short time after the boats came in the fishermen's wives or daughters would be on their way to town. Often barefoot, or wearing black sole-less stockings, as they crossed the moor, or, if the tide was out, took the short cut across the sands of Tong. And, on their backs, huge creels of prime haddocks kept fresh in a bed of grass.

When they got to town, kitchen doors would open gently, the well known cry would ring out, and the householders would buy the tastiest meal in the world, and at what a price. Six firm fresh haddocks for sixpence. Liver and all!

The fishwife's cry must have been my very first contact of all with Gaelic-speaking Lewis. I was familiar with it from earliest childhood, but I did not count it as Gaelic, because, until I had discovered that there was another Lewis, the fishwives and their cry were part of the Stornoway scene. I knew no other way of selling fish than opening a door and calling "An ceannaich sibh iasg?"

When one thinks of all the ceann cropic consumed in Lewis in these days, and the unrefined oatmeal, it is little wonder that Lewis was reputed to have the best teeth in Britain.

Just after the end of the Second World War a fishing boat from Point ran into trouble because of a dirty plug. According to Donald Matheson, the Bayble correspondent of the Gazette, an old stager who had gone with the crew for the trip, watched their unavailing struggle to unscrew the plug. He had no idea how the engine worked, but he saw what they were trying to do, tucked the outboard under his oxter, and loosened the plug with his teeth.

I'm not quite sure whether Donald was gently pulling my leg or not, but no one challenged the story when it did appear. The teeth of that generation were legendary.

A Stornoway business man who was addicted to smoking black twist once told me that when he went to a dentist in Glasgow he was told, "It's the best set of teeth I ever saw. And the dirtiest!"

A Carnegie Trust report in 1913 said the most striking feature of the adult population of Lewis was "their beautiful teeth", and, in 1940, Dr J. D. King reported that the teeth of school children in Lewis were markedly superior to those in most other parts of the U.K.

When his report was published I was asked for a story by the Daily Mail. I went along to see my cousin, Johnnie Matheson, who was a dentist in partnership with D. J. Macdonald on Kenneth Street. By chance, at the very moment I arrived, he had a septuagenarian from one of the villages in Pairc in the chair for his first extraction. He had broken a tooth on a bone!

Thirty years later, toothpaste containing fluoride was being distributed free in Lewis schools, in another experiment, because the island teeth were by then reputed to be the worst in Britain.

It is astonishing how much damage a modest dose of affluence can do in a single generation.

Sometimes, in addition to the haddocks in her creel, the fishwife would have eggs in a little wicker box with a hinged lid, which she carried in her hand. I would peer curiously into it when the lid was lifted, while my mother tried to make up her mind whether the eggs were really fresh, or whether they had been found in a corner of a harvest field where a broody hen had established a nest.

With the fish there was never any doubt. They were still almost swimming when you put them in the pot.

While the herring fishing was centred on Stornoway and prosecuted by well found drifters, most of them powered, the white fishing was still confined to small open boats, working from creeks and bays around the coast. It had to be that way for there were few harbours, and, even if there had been harbours there was no local market which could cope with the catch from a fleet of large vessels.

Round Broad Bay one of the richest fishing grounds in Britain, in proportion to its size, there was not a single pier, except at Tolsta, and that was in the wrong place, and of little use to anyone. Yet the whole population round the bay was dependent on fishing for their cash income.

Long before I was born, even before my father came to Lewis, the Walpole Committee recommended that a harbour should be constructed at Portnaguran.

It was built, or rather a pier was built, seventy years after the Committee reported, when the fishing was all but dead, and it was so constructed that it dries out at low tide.

All the belated expenditure achieved was to provide Lewis with a sour joke about the pier that was built ashore.

And even to get that far, that late, required a tremendous local effort in the raising of funds by voluntary subscription, to shame the authorities into action — a campaign in which the late John Macsween played a leading part.

During all the generations that Lewis depended on the fishing industry most of the fishermen, except a few who lived in favoured locations, had to manhandle their boats up and down the beaches every time they used them. Sometimes, in rough weather the women had to carry the men pick-a-back through the breakers so that they could begin the trip in dry clothes.

I have heard my father say that when he came to Lewis in the nineties it was practically unknown for a man from Ness, in the prime of life, to die in bed. If a Nessman escaped the ills of childhood he lived to a great age. Or was drowned at sea.

Shortly before my uncle Willie died, he sent me a copy of a report on the administration of the Ness Widows' and Orphans' Relief Fund from 1863 to 1874, which casts a sinister light on the social and economic facts that filled the folk memory, and conditioned the thinking, of the Lewis in which I grew up.

In December 1862, five boats left Port of Ness with thirty one men aboard. They were overtaken by a storm and none of them returned. They left twenty-four widows, seventy-one orphans, and thirty-one dependent relatives. Another seven children were born posthumously.

A fund of nearly £1500 was collected for the families, the contributors including Queen Victoria and the Prince of Wales. The treasurer of the fund was Donald Munro, the Chamberlain of Lewis.

In the first two years Munro made fairly substantial payments to the beneficiaries, but thereafter all the distributions were made on rent day.

As soon as a widow's portion was counted out she put her hand on the Chamberlain's pen in token of receipt. The money was then returned to his side of the table, and swept into the rent bag.

When challenged about his activities, Munro replied that he could not have applied the money more profitably for the widows than in payment of their rent, for, without their crofts they would have been destitute.

17
The Opium Trade and Ness Red Indians

Donald Munro, the Factor, did not get away with his cynical attempt to use the Ness disaster fund as insurance for his rents.

A London Lewisman, who had played a very active part in raising the Fund, exposed Munro's abuse of it.

When Munro became aware that his activities were coming under scrutiny, he set off hurriedly for Ness, in a snowstorm, with the whole balance of the Fund, in gold and silver, in a bag, and two revolvers in his pocket.

He carried the revolvers because he had heard that a party of crofters from Swainbost were marching on Stornoway to complain to the proprietor that he had unjustly deprived them of their grazings.

The astonished widows and dependents had nearly £600 distributed to them in a single windfall, and, according to Munro, they all signed a lengthy document in which they expressed their complete approval "of the Treasurer's intromissions" — a peculiar phrase for a group of "cailleachs" to use most of whom could neither read nor write, nor speak English.

The Report exposing Munro issued oddly enough, from the Oriental Club in London. It was compiled by W. D. Ryrie, who was presumably a member of the well known Stornoway family featured in Basil Lubbock's book on "The Opium Clippers."

Lubbock mentions three brothers, John, who was captain of the tea clippers *"Cairngorm"* and *"Flying Spur"*, Alexander who was captain of the opium schooner *"Sidney"*, and the *"Mazeppa"*, and Phineas, who was employed by a firm of merchants in Hong Kong.

W. D. Ryrie was, presumably, a cousin. Most of the Ryries had close connections with Jardine, Matheson & Co, the firm founded by Sir James Matheson, proprietor of Lewis and employer of Donald Munro, for whom W. D. Ryrie was gunning.

Ryrie's investigation of Munro's handling of the Fund seems to have begun around the time of Munro's exposure in Stornoway Sheriff Court during the trials arising from the so-called Bernera Riot.

He was alerted by a Mr Mackinlay, a contributor to the Fund, who was on a visit to Lewis about the time of the Bernera trial and heard accidentally that a large part of the Ness Fund was still lying in the bank. I have no idea who Mr Mackinlay was, but one of the witnesses at the trial of the Mutineers of the "Jane" half a century earlier was Peter McKinlay, "tidesman of Customs at Stornoway."

The man who activated Ryrie's inquiries might well have been like Ryrie himself, a member of one of the mainland families which have drifted in and out of Lewis history, making a greater contribution to the island's affairs than is perhaps generally recognised.

Munro attempted to defend his erratic handling of the Fund by explaining that some of the widows had remarried and their circumstances had changed. But that explanation would not hold.

The father of one of the drowned fishermen, John Macleod, aged 72 complained that he was destitute being unable to work at his trade of boat-building. He and his wife resided in part of a barn.

"All I have of stock is now two hens", he said. But Munro would give him nothing in the final division, although his claim was supported by Mr Kenneth Murray, a member of a Ness committee supposed to be advising on the administration of the Fund.

"None dare oppose the Factor", said Macleod. "I would have been content had I received of the last dividend as much as would buy a little clothing, or a pair of shoes, or even a stone of meal. But such would not be given me."

There is no suggestion that Munro misappropriated any of the Funds. Indeed when the money was finally paid out, the Central Committee, which Munro seems to have failed to consult over the years, accepted the Auditor's report, thanked Mr Munro for his services, and instructed that a copy of the accounts should be sent to Mr Ryrie.

This decision was taken by quite a formidable group including Sir James Matheson, and the two local doctors, Roderick Millar and Charles Macrae, both outstanding figures and men of probity.

Two members of the Committee, however, refused to support the motion on the ground that they did not have full information.

The two dissentients were Norman McIver who, I think, was a banker, and Rev. John McRae.

The impact of the disaster on Ness can be gauged from a report compiled by Rev. D. Macrae in January 1863. He writes, "Colin Macritchie, himself and his wife, aged people, had two sons, who lived with them, both drowned. One left a widow with three orphans, little girls. Other two widowed daughters belonging to the same family having five young children now fatherless.

"Another widow named Morison, whose husband, son, and son-in-law were all drowned some years ago, has, by the recent catastrophe, now lost her only surviving son, and also a son-in-law; so leaving three destitute widows and five orphans in one poor house; and, sad to say, with scarcely a potato to eat".

Other families, he added, were little better off.

"From marriage custom here, when a young man takes to himself a wife, he either takes her to his own father's house, or goes to live with her father, as the case may be; and therefore his labour is the mainstay and support of the household. Old men cannot prosecute the ling fishing off the Butt in the very mouth of the Northern side of the stormy Atlantic. The backbone, for a time, of our fishermen is broken."

And Ryrie concluded his own Report with the significant sentence, "in that peaty wilderness of an island there is always recurring and lamentable destitution to be relieved; and within the last three months two boats' crews of fishermen have gone to their rest leaving widows and orphans in as destitute and unshielded a condition as any of the recipients from the Ness Fund."

Many years later one of the orphans whose interests Ryrie was trying to protect became well known in the North West territory of Canada as Moccasin Bill. He was a son of Finlay Mackenzie of Habost, and he earned his nickname because once, when he was in danger of starving when out trapping, he kept himself alive by eating his snowboots.

In going to Canada, Moccasin Bill was following a family tradition: his uncle was one of the survivors of the Riel Rebellion.

I never met either of the Mackenzies, but I learned of them through John Macaskill of Garden Road, who fished Lake Winnipeg from a base at Eagle Island with Moccasin Bill, before coming back to Lewis to work in Bain and Morrison's woodyard, and become one of the pioneers of trade unionism in the Western Isles.

A lean wiry man, with a stoop and a sallow complexion, as if he was in perpetual ill health, John Macaskill was an honest, upright, hard-working Socialist of the old school. A man I came to admire immensely although I did not share his views.

He was picking up his fishing boat once at Bull Harbour on Lake Winnipeg with Moccasin Bill when a flotilla of Indian canoes drew in crammed with men women and children, who swarmed ashore and began to erect their tents about fifty yards from the boats.

A tall black-bearded man left the Indian camp and walked over to the two Lewismen. To Macaskill's astonishment the "Indian" spoke to them in Gaelic.

He was Bill's uncle who had married a Red Indian. His squaw was with him, with their sons, daughters and grandchildren.

18
Rebellion, Oysters, and a Son of Dickens

Ness was not the only part of Lewis which had close connections with Hudson's Bay last century.

The mention of Moccasin Bill brings back to mind the soft brown moccasins that used to lie with the boots and shoes in my grannie's cupboard when I was a child.

They fascinated me, but it never occurred to me to ask who had brought them home. I accepted them as part of the furniture of the house just as the modern child accepts the telephone and television.

They might have been brought home by my grandfather from one of his voyages, like the brightly coloured glass bead necklaces from Africa which used to hang beside the parlour chimney.

But that raises other questions. Were the African beads really brought home by my grandfather, or were they brought home at a later date by my uncle when he visited the Church of Scotland missions in Africa on behalf of the General Assembly?

How can I really know the island when simple facts about my own close relatives elude me?

I am reminded too that among my books there is a manuscript diary my uncle kept during that African tour. So far I have not got round to reading it. Is this something else that must be explored?

And welling up from memory comes the thought that the moccasins were brought home by my grannie's brother-in-law, Captain John Smith, or more likely by one of his brothers, who had been to Hudson's Bay. Did I really hear that as a child or is it just a guess by a wildly groping mind?

At the end of last century the northern territory of Canada was almost an extension of Lewis so many men went out as trappers. The Hudson's Bay Company retained the services of a doctor in Stornoway at that time to screen recruits for the company's services.

The Riel Rebellions of 1869 and 1885, in which the French-Indian Metis, or half breeds, rose in defence of their language and their lands, are almost part of Lewis history, so many islanders were caught up in the swirl.

One who is remembered is Big Bear Maclean from Uig. He got his nickname because his friendship with an Indian chief, Big Bear, enabled him to save the life of a son of Charles Dickens.

Inspector Dickens of the Canadian Mounties was surrounded at Fort Pitt by five hundred Indians and Metis. He had only a handful of men, but he had to make a stand for the sake of the civilians in the Fort.

Maclean, who was also in Fort Pitt with his wife and family, went out to negotiate on the strength of his friendship with the Indian chief.

When the negotiations were in progress one of Riel's runners, a bloodthirsty

Indian known as Wandering Spirit, arrived on the scene, and demanded that Maclean should place his wife and family in the Indians' hands as hostages.

It was a difficult decision, but Maclean knew that, if they tried to defend the Fort, they would all eventually be massacred. The Indians were planning to burn it down that night.

He wrote a letter to his wife, asking her and the other trappers' families, to join him in the Indian camp.

Once the civilians were in Indian hands, there was no purpose in defending the Fort. Inspector Dickens and his men slipped quietly down the river under the cover of darkness, to safety at Battleford. It was not an easy journey. Their boat was leaking, and there was running ice in the river.

When the Rebellion was suppressed, it was found that Fort Pitt had been looted and burned, but the Macleans and the other civilians were unharmed, although they suffered some privations while in Indian hands.

So far as I know, Big Bear Maclean did not return to Lewis, but, unless my memory is playing me tricks, it was his brother who worked the oyster beds at Gisla when I was a boy, and who once sold several dozen, on the same day, to Lord Leverhulme and to Willie John Tolmie, the chemist, at widely different prices.

Willie John, who told me the story, thought, and I agreed, that it was a very civilised adjustment of the market price to accord to the customers' bank accounts.

I have no idea whether Big Bear Maclean's wife was a Lewiswoman, or whether she was an Indian. She might have been either.

The first white woman to go down the Athabaska River to Fort Chipewyan by canoe was an eighteen year old bride from Tong. She went out in 1880 to join her trapper husband, James Thomson, with a label round her neck to tell her name and destination.

She made the journey safely, despite the fact that for 1500 miles of it, shooting rapids and negotiating portages, she was encumbered with a crate containing six hens and a cockerel given her at Fort Carlton by Ross Macfarlane, a Stornoway man.

She and her husband eventually returned to Lewis, and for many years we bought our winter fuel from them, although, as a child, I had no idea that the "sgiobalt" little bodach who came to us once a year with a load of peats had ever been out of the island.

On the other hand, quite a number of Lewismen who went to the "talamh fuar" married Indians, and some eventually came back to Lewis with their wives. The wives seem to have been assimilated into Lewis as readily and as completely as Finlay Mackenzie's uncle from Ness was assimilated into his Indian tribe.

And they brought new and valuable qualities into the island with them. At least, as boys, we had no doubt where the prowess of Roddie Mackay, the legendary Wedger, derived from.

Possibly the finest athlete the island has produced, he was still unchallenged at the pole vault at an age when most folk are thinking of wheel chairs.

His ease and grace at the games in Willowglen are one of my abiding memories, but I remember him, too, in quite another connection.

One night, when I was walking through Laxdale with some of my school pals, we met him and got talking politics. It would have been in the middle twenties, around the time of the National Strike, when poverty and unemployment were rife in the island, on a scale it is almost impossible to visualise today.

Wedger felt very strongly about the state of the country and the island. As we parted he said to us, "If I had your education I would be hanging from that lamp-post".

There was no lamp-post in sight, as it happened, but his meaning was clear.

We left him, a little startled by the realisation that education has obligations as well as opportunities.

I have never forgotten the incident, or the moral, although I have always held the view that there are more effective ways of bringing about social change than getting oneself strung up from a lamp-post. Although perhaps, that course has the greatest precedent of all.

Significantly Wedger did not suggest hanging other people from lamp-posts. He was talking about self-sacrifice not violence.

19
The Day I Killed the Kaiser

I was very happy in my early years at school. It was, as I have said, almost an extension of the family circle.

I don't think I had any special privileges. At least I was never conscious of any, or tempted to trade on my position, which in a small community was necessarily shared by many of my classmates who had their own similar, but separate, links with our teachers.

But, when I was off school, my class teacher was sufficiently interested to come round to the house to see whether I was seriously ill. It rather terrified me to see her sitting there with my mother at the fireside. Was it really a mission of peace, or was I suspected of malingering?

My teacher, at that time, was one of the Millar's from just along the street. Her sister was married to Murdo Morrison from Tong who became the legendary Director of Education of Inverness-shire. It was said that he knew every pupil in the vast county, and, long after his retirement, when he was a centenarian he divided his daily reading between English and French, and kept up a voluminous correspondence, in an immaculate hand, with a host of correspondents.

Sometimes, in the summer, when the Morrison boys were in Stornoway on holiday I played with them in the garden at the back of the Millars' home. School and family were almost one.

In the same way, and for the same reason, when a few years later, I wrote an outrageous essay on what I would do with £100, news of it quickly percolated back to my mother, and I was teased relentlessly, albeit gently.

The result is that a school exercise, which would otherwise have been forgotten the moment it was written, has remained in my memory, accusingly, reminding me of the journalist's (or incipient journalist's) cardinal sin — over simplification!

My teacher then was Kathleen Harrold, who later married my cousin Willie Pope and spent most of her married life in Vancouver. She was a lovely woman, with a nature to match, but she did laugh heartily over the facility with which I stretched my £100 from such small, but important, matters as the purchase of jumbaballs, to the acquisition of a submarine, in which I made my way to Germany, and killed the Kaiser.

The War — the Kaiser War — conditioned everything in our young lives.

It was always held against me that, when I was refused something I desperately wanted, with the promise "You'll get it after the war," I broke into tears and asked despairingly "Will there ever be an after the war?" There was, but it was very different from what anyone expected.

It was the War which first made me really conscious of the outside world to which all the busy shipping in the harbour plied.

Before that, the outside world had been homogenous, all of it, because Lewis was real and it was not. I knew, in a vaguely intellectual way, that Lewis was part of something called Britain, and I had once been on the mainland as far as Inverness, but I was too young at the time to have any recollection of it.

Until the war, the world consisted of just two places, Lewis and not Lewis. But once the war broke out I became conscious of nationality. Of the existence of other individual countries with characteristics of their own.

I believed, like most other British children brought up during the Kaiser War, that Britain (unreal though it still was to me) was different from all other countries, because it was not only the best and most powerful, and the bravest, but even that it was completely immaculate — a belief strangely at variance with the doctrine of Original Sin which I learned by rote from the Shorter Catechism, and which sat heavily upon me every Sunday in church.

Except, of course, the Sunday when I gave original sin its head, squatted on the floor in a tantrum, and thrust my hand up the leg of my brother's trousers to tickle him, because he had taken my favourite corner seat.

I disorganised the service almost as completely as I had done on my very first day in church some years before. On that earlier occasion I announced the arrival of everyone I recognised, in a voice that boomed through the building, and generally by their nicknames, which were not always polite.

Finally, when my old nurse maid, dear kindly Katie Ann, arrived, I leant forward to the pew where she was sitting to plant a smacker on her cheek. I often wondered, when I sat at meetings of the Lewis Association, many years later, with her husband, the "Duke," from Bernera, whether he knew that I had been in love with his wife, long before she ever knew him?

The difference between my two escapades in church was that, on the second occasion, I got the only thrashing I can recall — and it was truly memorable — because I was assumed to have come to years of discretion, whereas, on the first occasion, my mother merely whispered to me that the service was over, and whisked me quickly out of the church before it had even begun.

We had gone on that occasion to my uncle's church, the High, instead of to our own, and having heard me greet Murdo Macrae, the butcher, so vociferously, and Katie Ann so affectionately, my mother was terrified to think what might happen when I saw my uncle emerge from the varnished door with the little glass panels, at the end of the church, dressed, as I had never seen him before, in his long black gown, and Geneva bands, and ascend the pulpit.

My recollection is that that adventure in church was at night. My father and brother had gone away some days before to spend a holiday at my paternal grandmother's in Inverness. My mother and I were to follow on the Sunday night, and she had taken me to church to fill the evening in until the steamer sailed. It was probably the excitement of the journey in prospect which overcame my natural shyness, and made me so demonstrative.

I see my grandfather's cottage frequently, now that I am resident in Inverness. It still stands between Tomnahurich Cemetery and the Caledonian Canal, although it has been outwardly changed by the addition of some gaily coloured garden figures which did not exist when I knew it first.

But I remember very little of the holiday itself. Except the thrill of being allowed to stand on the swing bridge while it was being opened by the lock-keepers to permit the passage of a ship.

I also have a vague recollection of getting into a stage coach — it must have been at Fort Augustus — after a journey down Loch Ness by boat, which I have quite forgotten.

At this point memory, reinforced by the family, embarrassingly, over the years, informs me gently that my behaviour in church was not an aberration under stress or excitement, as I have represented it to be, for, in the hotel in Fort Augustus, where we lunched, I pointed an accusing finger at a commercial traveller, innocently filling his glass from a carafe at the next table, and announced to the dining room at large, "That man is drinking all the water."

And that was probably the incipient journalist's most natural gesture — the easy accusing finger at other people's lapses, or imagined lapses.

But this requires a postscript.

By the oddest of coincidences, just after I had written it I received, out of the blue, a letter from my old nurse, now living with her daughter near Dounreay. And in her letter she recalled the incident in church I have been describing.

Thought transference? I wonder!

Anyway her account confirms my recollection. In fact she adds to it.

Having announced the arrival of Murdo Macrae, the butcher, who was an elder in the church, I extended the same courtesy to Johnny "Oak", the baker, another elder.

And when my mother carried me out protesting, I demanded my money back!
I knew I was missing the show I came to see!

20
Camouflage and a Private World

Although I had been to the mainland quite early in life, and knew that my father's parents lived there, it was still remote and separate. I belonged to Lewis and to no where else.

Even to this day I belong to Lewis in a way I have never belonged to Britain or even Scotland: in the sense of being possessed by a place, not merely acknowledging, in an objective way, that I was born and nurtured there.

Lewis, to me, is not part of Britain. It is not even an island lying off the British coast. It is a community complete in itself, with a neighbour lying across the Minch, often obscured by rain, but sometimes clear along the skyline in blue serrated summits, or snow-capped peaks, glowing apricot or pink in the winter sun.

The rest of Britain is an extension of Lewis, the second circle of endlessly recurring and expanding but diminishing waves, which mark the centre where the stone was thrown into the pool.

No one who has not lived for a great part of his life on an island can possibly understand the intensity of this love of place.

I have frequently been taken aback, in conversation with intelligent and sensitive people, to hear them express surprise at the parochial attachment to place they have found in small remote communities. It has required a real mental effort for me to adjust to the fact that it is the islander's commitment which is unusual rather than other peoples' detachment.

In our mobile fluent civilisation in which the world has become a single village, and people move rapidly from place to place and from job to job in furtherance of their personal careers, the islander's attachment to his birthplace is an anachronism, an aberration. But that very fact may make it more significant, and, perhaps, more important, than it has ever been.

The idea that the future of mankind is best served when the individual's only commitment is to the pursuit of his own career requires the same sort of qualification as the belief that the free play of market forces will produce the best possible world for all.

It is a comforting illusion that, if everyone maximises his own personal success, the sum total of success will be greater than if we let ourselves be held back by other considerations. But I doubt it.

It is not necessarily true that one man's success is another man's failure, but there is sufficient truth in it to expose the hollow myth that a free-wheeling, competitive society will produce either greater happiness for all, or even greater material prosperity for all, than a society regulated on other principles.

Belonging to an island is very different from belonging to a club, a society, a party, or even a church.

All these groupings are based, to some extent at least, on identity of beliefs or interests. They are exclusive of those who do not share them.

Attachment to place can be exclusive, too, in the sense that we separate ourselves from other places, but it also means that we accept as members of the same community all who belong to our own place whether we agree with them or not. A fellow islander is a fellow islander even if we hate his guts. As much part of the community as we are ourselves.

Indeed in a closely knit community like an island we are as tightly bound to the people we dislike as to the people we love. They, just as surely, help to establish our identity and define our place in the whole. It is this sense of knowing where one fits in that modern man is in danger of losing.

Even absence does not necessarily diminish one's attachment to a place if it is clearly identified to begin with. In fact absence may intensify the attachment because it idealises the object we are attached to.

Lewis has benefited greatly from the continuing interest of those who have left, but at times it has suffered. The late Stephen MacLean once commented shrewdly on the damage done, during the Leverhulme era by emigre Lewismen, still interested in the island, articulate and outspoken, but able to take a romantic view. They were fighting to preserve an Eden which had never existed, while those who remained at home had to grapple with the realities of a very imperfect world.

I did not choose to remain in Lewis, attached to it though I was. Circumstances held me there, and, at times, I was an unwilling prisoner. But having spent the greater part of my life on the island, I am in no danger of romanticising it. I flatter myself, however, that sitting at my desk in Inverness, looking out on the Moray Firth and the fresh snow on Ben Wyvis, I can write of it with greater objectivity than when I was in Stornoway in the thick of events.

As I have already indicated, I was aware from a very early age that, as part of the Anglicised and Anglicising Stornoway establishment, I was a stranger looking in, rather than myself an integral part of the Lewis community. This unusual and uneasy balance between exclusion and involvement has limited my knowledge of Lewis, in some respects, but has sharpened my understanding.

I became aware of my own situation when I moved into the Secondary school and found myself for the first time in a class where the majority of the pupils were Gaelic-speakers, who could withdraw at any moment into a private world to which I had no entry.

They never deliberately embarrassed me by using Gaelic to shut me out, and their English was better than my own. But, having thought of rural Lewis up until then, in terms of black houses, and fishermen, barefoot women hawking haddocks from door to door, and gangling youths on Market Day with droves of sheep, I now found myself in the company of boys and girls from these same villages who were in every aspect of life — physical, intellectual and moral — my equals, and often my superiors.

In the holidays I sometimes saw the girls of my class, their modest finery set aside, barefoot on the moor with a creel of peats, or the boys, herding the sheep or working the boats, absorbed into their old environment as completely as if they had been camouflaged by nature to conceal the fact that they were no longer part of the egalitarian crofting village, although not yet ready to take wing and leave it for good.

59

The concealment may even have been deliberate, because they had their own loyalty to the closed community of the village to which they belonged, and were slow to separate themselves from the friends who were not graduating with them out of the village and into the professions.

Today town and country are almost indistinguishable but sixty years ago it was very different.

When I was a child at school, three families out of four in rural Lewis lived in thatched houses, and in the years of unemployment, and crop failure, just after the First World War, Helen Porter, the MOH, commented bitterly, in one of her reports, that in a rural Lewis school you could often pick out the children of war widows from the rest, because they were better shod and clad. It was not that the wars widows' pensions were princely, but many other families at that time had even less.

Dr Porter's comments were taken up by "John Bull", somewhat distorted and exaggerated. There was great indignation among the good folk of the town who regarded poverty as a stigma, and had no wish to be associated with it.

I was aware of the commotion because these things were freely discussed at table, and my father, as the only local journalist, was always at the centre of any conflict between what was actually happening and what people wanted to hear.

Piquancy was added to the situation because Dr Porter was then on the point of marrying Hugh Miller, the District Clerk, an apparently confirmed bachelor, a close friend of the family, and the official spokesman of the Council in which the battle between those who wanted to play up the island's poverty for political reasons and those who wanted to play it down for personal pride was raging most fiercely.

21
The Redhead's Riddle

By the townsmen of my childhood, in fact by all townsmen in all ages, a rural background and a minority language are regarded as stigmata of an inferior culture.

But the ease with which my classmates in the Nicolson moved between two quite different environments, and the academic distinction which so many of them achieved, were evidence enough that they brought from their homes, and their oral Gaelic tradition, qualities at least as valuable as those acquired through English from the schools.

Some of my classmates were more thoroughly Anglicised than I was, because they never came to regret what they had lost, including some who belonged to families not long removed from a rural Gaelic background, and still busily shedding the last distinctive features of their personality.

There was another group — the children of country families which had moved into town in search of work, but were still in their language and their attitudes, part of rural Lewis, not yet assimilated to the town or consciously seeking assimilation.

It was one of these, a girl whose name I have forgotten, but whose burnished copper hair still glows across the years, as it used to glow across the passage between our desks, unkempt but splendid, who first put to me the riddle, "What equals four and a half?", and the answer "A piggy in a bag."

It was a riddle which encapsulated a situation which conditioned a good deal of my childhood, and has greatly influenced my adult views.

There was a long history of crusading, evangelistic, prohibitionism in Stornoway.

At one time it was the annual custom for the Lewis Justices to withdraw all the liquor licenses in town when they came up for renewal. The decision was always reversed, a few weeks later, by the Appeal Court in Dingwall, as everyone knew it would be when the original decision was taken.

This, however, was an admirable arrangement. It enabled the local justices to enjoy all the satisfaction of a moral stand without having to face the consequences of their decision.

They could bask in the esteem of the temperance faction — if temperance is the word — without quarrelling too seriously with their publican friends. And at the end of the day they were left with the sweetest of all consolations — a grievance against the nabobs of Easter Ross, whose colonial government of Lewis was bitterly, and often with justice, resented.

It was during this period that a prominent citizen, pressed for his views on the matter at a public meeting, replied, equivocally, "I am in favour of putting down the drink!"

He was! His periodic bouts of delirium tremens, alternating with long periods of complete sobriety, were one of the open secrets of the town, spoken of with a mixture of amusement, sympathy and disapprobation.

The proportion of ingredients in the mixture might vary from person to person, but the three were almost always there. Stornoway was critical of its public figures, but it was also tolerant, so long as they followed the role in which the community had cast them or had come to accept them. What pleasure would our saints have had without our sinners to gloat over?

The British Women's Temperance Association, the Band of Hope, and the Good Templars were all active in the town. Before my time there appears to have been a Good Templars Lodge in the school as well. No trace of it remained in my day except an ancient certificate of incorporation, or affiliation, hanging on one of the classroom walls.

I never really knew the history of the school Lodge, or why it was disbanded. The faded parchment had become so much a part of the room it had no more significance than a patch of damp, or a spot where the plaster was peeling from the walls. Most of the dingy classrooms had examples of both!

I don't know either what were the activities, if any, of the Band of Hope, beyond the holding of an annual soiree, which I was not permitted to attend. In my parents' view some of the boys who went to the soiree were too rough for me, which suggests that, in my childhood, I must have been a sensitive plant, or mollycoddled.

It was said that some of the bigger boys would persuade a youngster to rise from his seat on some pretext, and slip a broken cup below him to see what happened when he sat. But I never heard of anyone being hurt, and I suspect there was more bombast than brutality in the behaviour of the boys.

Most of them, not surprisingly, were there for what they could scran, to use the colloquial term, and their presence had nothing to do with their future sobriety.

When the Local Option clause of the 1913 Scottish Temperance Act became operative in 1920, however, Stornoway's charade was at an end. Prohibition became a live issue, and a lively one!

My father was a prohibitionist. I never saw alcohol in any form in our home, except on one occasion when my uncle was seriously ill and the doctor prescribed champagne.

There was quite a family council of war before it was decided that I, then in my last year at school, should go to the Royal Hotel and make the purchase.

The hotelier was most helpful. He gave me a little tap by which the champagne could be drawn off, as required, without opening the bottle. But, when I got home, we had a visitor. I left the bottle discreetly in the kitchen, saying nothing about it until I had seen the visitor safely home through the dark. By that time my father had uncorked the bottle, in an effort to be helpful, and spoiled the lot!

I don't know whether we got another bottle. I certainly was not sent for one. Or whether my uncle recovered without recourse to strong drink.

He certainly would have preferred it that way because he was one of the leaders of the No Licence Campaign.

He had worked as a youth, for a short time, in a public house owned by his uncle Colin, and his views on alcohol were deeply rooted in what he learned then of the damage it can do.

Though passionate and unbending in his hatred of the trade, he had sufficient sense of humour to laugh when, with a friend who shared his views, he once ate his

62

trifle in a Glasgow restaurant with so much relish that he asked for a second helping, whereupon the waiter said, "It ought to be good today — the sherry bottle slipped!"

At a crowded Temperance Rally in the Drill Hall my uncle eloquently compared the noise from the Imperial Bar with the roar of Broad Bay on a winter night.

It is a comparison which is probably meaningless today. The extension of the town, the noise of the traffic, and the fact that people are seldom abroad at night except in cars, have shut us off from what was at one time one of the most characteristic sounds of Stornoway. The great sustained tumult which enveloped the place when there was a strong easterly wind driving the breakers on to the beaches from Aignish, Melbost and Stenish round to Coll and Gress. It was a noise you didn't hear but feel.

The audience at that meeting in the twenties saw the point my uncle was making, but the effect was destroyed by a beery voice from the back of the hall, "Shud up or you'll no have a preach for Sunday!"

We adopted the phrase in the family as a convenient way of breaking off an argument when it was going against us.

22
An Odd Habit in a Windy Town

The year 1920, when the first no-licence poll was held, was an exciting one in Stornoway.

The meetings of the prohibition party had all the fervour of a great revival. I was so carried away by the vehemence of those who were wrestling with "the demon drink" that I remained a prohibitionist myself for many years.

At University my priggish attitude to the social habits of most of my contemporaries must have been a bit offensive although I tried to sweeten my criticism with a touch of humour.

It was later I came to realise that many of the devils we wrestle with in this life — political even more than religious — are invented by ourselves, so that we can dodge the much more difficult task of understanding complex issues and really trying to solve them.

In 1920, however, it was easy to imagine that I was one of a great army of crusaders marching towards the sound of gunfire. Or that I would have been if I had been old enough to have a vote. It was exhilarating even to be on the sidelines. In fact it was almost as intoxicating as the spirit we condemned. And perhaps more dangerous because it made us self-righteous.

The first Poll took place just about the time I moved into the Secondary Department, and found myself a neighbour of the red haired lass, who posed me the problem of the "piggy in a bag."

It has come back to me that her name was Kennedy, which suggests that the family had come into town from one of the villages of Pairc.

When the votes were counted there was a thumping majority for Prohibition and every bar in the town was closed. Stornoway was dry. At least in theory!

There were, of course, shebeens. I have no idea how many. But years later one of the leading citizens of the town told me that he had only to hang a towel from his bathroom window, when the town was reputedly dry, and a bottle of whisky would be delivered to him within the hour.

There may have been a bit of exaggeration in that, as there undoubtedly was in the reports which circulated from time to time of police raids on private houses, which failed to reveal anything because the illicit spirits were concealed in pianos, and other unlikely spots, with an ingenuity unequalled even in "Whisky Galore".

But there were real raids and real arrests.

The premises of Alex Jamieson, a general dealer with a store in Bells Road who played a prominent part in the sporting life of the island, were raided from time to time.

During one of the raids Jamieson's book-keeper turned faint. She had to lie down while he fetched her some hot milk.

A suspicious policeman had her removed from the bench on which she was reclining, and beneath it he found a considerable cache of spirits.

Later there was a learned legal argument in the Court as to whether it was more than could be considered appropriate for a man to have, on his own premises, for his own use.

The police, on that occasion, showed considerable diligence, but I have a feeling that, perhaps with more sense than the victorious Prohibition Party, they were not too anxious to close every little leakage, provided things did not get out of hand.

My father was subject to considerable pressure during this period as the proprietor of the only local paper in the island. He could have waxed prosperous on the advertising he was offered by mainland firms anxious to slake the thirst of Stornoway by post.

He could have done with the money. At that time the "Gazette" was printed on the mainland, by his brothers, and he carried out the whole editorial and reporting work with a staff of one — a diligent and faithful book-keeper. His earnings from the paper were minimal and he eked them out by part-time work as a meteorologist, shorthand writer to the courts, and teacher of commercial subjects in the school.

He resisted the temptation to profit by the town's decision to close the pubs, but when the first three years of the great experiment were up, and a new poll was called for, he opened the columns of the paper to "the trade" in the belief that the voters had a right to hear both sides of the argument before coming to a decision.

This nice distinction was not understood by some of the stalwarts in the Prohibition camp — in spite of the fact that they got their advertising for nothing while their opponents paid for theirs. It was then, for the first time in my life, I made the acquaintance of the anonymous poison pen letter. He was a traitor to the cause!

My mother was distressed by these attacks. My father almost enjoyed them. In a way this was surprising, because my mother was normally the more resilient of the two.

Indeed, when he threw up his job as reporter for the "Highland News" to found the "Gazette" — a serious gamble for a man with no capital behind him and a young family to provide for — she insisted on posting his letter of resignation, so that he could not reproach himself afterwards if things went wrong.

The shebeens and the postal trade were of small account during Stornoway's dry spell. The Lewis Hotel, whether by prescience or chance, had a wholesale licence and that was not affected by the poll! They were quite within the law in continuing to trade, provided they sold not less than four and a half gallons of beer at a time.

So the custom grew up among the dockers, and others, of clubbing together for a "four and a half" — the "piggy in a bag" of my redhead's riddle.

Sometimes, no doubt, the beer was carried in a "piggy", but normally it was carried in a large tin can. It was taken to a quiet corner of the quay, or, if the tide was out, down one of the "slants" where the deck of the pier afforded cover.

The temperance folk glowered at the "four and a halfs" and grumbled at the law which made a farce of their victory.

The more respectable would-be drinkers looked on a little enviously because they could not stoop to public drinking with a "school" of dockers — "School" was the phrase in common use, inappropriate though it may seem.

The police, when the mood was on them, or under pressure from the temperance lobby, watched furtively, from behind the herring barrels, in the hope that they would see money passing, which would transform the "school" into an open air shebeen.

Occasionally they swooped on Tolas, or some other potential victim, and carefully measured the contents of the tin, in the hope that a dent in the side, or short measure by the publican, had reduced the contents below the legal minimum.

They got very few convictions, but provided quite a lot of amusement in the Courts, as when Sheriff Haldane, a dry, rather pompous man, who looked like Woodrow Wilson, asked a docker how much he had had to drink, and received the unabashed reply, "You'll just have to split four and a half by six. I'm not the best scholar here."

And so the Woods of Edinburgh, who owned Lewis Hotel, continued to prosper (legally) from the sale of liquor in a dry town, and the inhabitants of one of the rainiest and windiest parts of Britain developed an odd habit of alfresco drinking, which they have never completely abandoned, although the practice is now confined to the odd screwtop, in a doorway, after permitted hours.

23
The Kipper Fell In The Fire

During the six years that Stornoway was dry the hotels deteriorated badly. There was not enough revenue to sustain them without the bars.

On one occasion a weary traveller arrived at the Caledonian Hotel, late at night, from the mail steamer. He was given the choice of a kipper or a boiled egg for supper.

He opted for the kipper, but, after an inordinate wait, he was served the egg.

"The kipper fell in the fire!" said the waitress, perfunctorily. It had been the only one in the house.

The Imperial, the largest of the Hotels, and the one which had inspired my uncle's oratory, was sold. It became the first school hostel associated with the Nicolson, and, if I mistake not, the first school hostel anywhere in Scotland, serving a public school. A public school that is, in the Scottish (and logical) sense of that much abused term.

The hostel was badly needed because digs for the country boys and girls were hard to come by, and grossly overcrowded, especially in the fishing season.

Not long ago two Nicolsonians of my own vintage were recalling the cramped conditions in which they lived and studied in Stornoway digs.

They had to buy their own provisions but the rent they paid the landlady covered the cooking. At the week end, five schoolboys went each to his favourite butcher to buy a bit of mutton for the Sunday broth.

The broth for all five was cooked in the one pot, but each had a little piece of string, with his own private knot, attached to his mutton, so that he could identify it again when it was finally fished out.

One of the things which troubled the authorities was the risk that boys and girls might be accommodated in the same house.

There was a story told that on one occasion when Mr Gibson, the Rector, was making a tour of inspection of some of the lodgings, an awkward situation was averted by the quick thinking of the landlady's daughter, herself a pupil.

The Rector asked about some boys he understood were lodging there. She directed him, through a narrow close, to the back door of the same house, where one of her parents, whom he did not know, met him, and showed him in.

These shifts were necessary. They were part of the cost of survival at a time when most people in Scotland, and children from the rural areas of the Hebrides in particular, purchased their education by very considerable sacrifices on their part, and the part of their families. And valued it accordingly!

In a very much later era when a school hostel was built in Tarbert the authorities were liberal minded enough to accommodate boys and girls in the same building. Of course they made sure there was pretty solid door between the two dormitories. It was only when the hostel was built they realised it was a fire door which could never be locked.

I don't think any harm resulted.

The Louise Carnegie Girls' Hostel was perhaps the only benefit which Stornoway derived from the noble, but misguided experiment in prohibition. And even that would no doubt have come in due season, even if the Imperial had not been on the market.

For myself, I lost one of my best friends, when the Imperial was sold — Bunty Carnegie, the proprietor's son.

So far as I know there was no connection whatsoever between the Carnegies who sold the hotel, and the Louise Carnegie after whom the hostel was called. In fact the coincidence of the names never struck me until now.

Oddly almost my only recollection of Bunty is of him singing, it must have been at a school concert, or a soiree of some sort,

> *For I kissd her on the ship,*
> *And the crew began to roar,*
> *Ailie O. Ailie O,*
> *For we're off to Baltimore.*

An incongruous song surely for a ten year old. But why then has it stuck in my memory?

When the family left Lewis he passed completely out of my life, but I used to see one of his older sisters occasionally. She married a Channel Islander named Quenet, who was in the fish trade and visited Stornoway fairly regularly for many years.

He was a very good golfer, but rather irascible, and with a remarkable vocabulary of ingenious expletives, which gave rise to a number of stories, some possibly true, some certainly apocryphal, which as boys we listened to with bated breath in the professional's shop.

On one occasion a minister with whom he was playing is said to have abandoned the match at the third hole remarking "I am reasonably broad minded but I draw the line when my opponent calls on The Almighty to commit an indecent act on his ball".

Old Bob MacIntosh, the professional, of whom I was very fond, had a notably pungent turn of phrase himself, and no doubt fathered some of his own inventions on Quenet.

Anyway it was all part of my education, and one of the joys of life.

In this permissive age when the foulest language is used on television in the name of realism (or freedom) we have deprived ourselves of a great and harmless pleasure. In fact of a therapy.

A forbidden language, which can only be used clandestinely, is an important safety valve, especially when young boys are passing through the most difficult phase of growing up.

The apostles of liberty, by trying to defuse the swear word and render it acceptable have deprived themselves of a pleasure similar to poaching, and simultaneously imposed on other people a vocabulary which gives genuine and deep offence.

It was much the same lesson which Stornoway learned in another context, when, after six years of No Licence, the townsfolk decided that they had had enough.

Prohibition had not put an end to drunkenness. It had simultaneously driven drink underground, and into the open. It encouraged hypocrisy and law breaking. There was almost nothing to commend it.

But when the bars were opened up again, (except of course, the Imperial,) and new bars and hotels were built, the town settled down to learn the hard way that the problems arising from the abuse of alcohol cannot be solved by permissiveness any more than by prohibition.

It is a dilemma we share with almost every community on earth, and which, in our own case, has been compounded in recent years, by a relative affluence, which is to be preferred to the poverty of the period of which I write, but with which we have not yet learned to cope, in some respects, at least.

Writing to the Commissioners of the Forfeited Estates in 1721, to assure them that Lewis was "disciplined into passive obedience", Zachary Macaulay, the Factor, added, "But I can assure yee shall find one rugged hag that will resist both King and Government vizt. Poverty."

The rugged hag has been the island's pretty constant companion over the years, but I thought of her as a ghost rather than a reality the last time I was home, and saw, at a modest reckoning, round a rural church, on a Sunday evening, more than a quarter of a million pounds worth of motor cars.

It was a change which would have astonished not only my grandmother, but my mother, and she died just thirty years ago.

In fact, it astonishes me.

24
The Omnipresent Millionaire

Although we were conscious of the "four and a halfs" when we sneaked across the pier to steal a herring for bait without the cooper seeing us, so that we could fish for cuddies from the stone steps opposite the Waverley Hotel, or when we tried to "walk" a barrel along the pier, by rotating it with our feet, balancing as best we could against the barrel's tendency to wobble, we were not really curious, or even interested.

The "four and a halfs" were part of the landscape. It seemed the most natural thing in the world, we were so familiar with it, that men should be seen in little groups in corners here and there, drinking beer from large tin cans.

We might pass a comment about the people in the "school", if we recognised any of the local characters round whom our conversation otherwise revolved.

Like Anga, the red faced docker, with the huge spade hands, thrust out in front of him like miniature snowploughs, as he moved along with a stiff ungainly gait. We spoke of him a lot because on every conceivable occasion he asked us boys, "Have you got a sister?", a question, which caused us great hilarity, coming from such a source, and because of its titillating implications.

Or Tolas, the gentle drunkard, with the great brown pleading eyes, which made my mother speak of Murray Beaton (she always used his correct name) with pity and affection, as if he were still one of her pupils — as in physical size he might have been. She seemed to feel an urge to shield him from a world, which I think she foresaw even in his childhood, would deal harshly with one so ill-equipped for the only type of employment open to him in Stornoway — that of a dockside carter.

If anything did distract our attention from whatever serious business of our own we had in hand, it was more likely to be the arrival of a vessel we had never seen before. Or a drifter down by the bows with a miraculous draught of fishes.

Or a basking shark entangled in herring nets, and dumped on the South Beach, a vast slimy corpse draped incongruously with what looked like brown lace, but which in fact represented a large part of the capital of a hard hit crew.

Or it might be the waving of a red flag in the Castle Grounds across the Bay, and a scampering of men for cover, before the spurt of smoke and flying stones, followed some moments later by the laggard sound of the explosion, as Lord Leverhulme's navvies blasted out of the solid rock the road that was to link the old town of Stornoway with the new town on Arnish Point. A town which filled his dreams and ours, but which was never built, although half a century later, the same site was chosen for the same reasons, by Lewis Offshore for building oil rigs.

The Marina, to give the new road the pretentious name used in the Estate records, replaced the narrow path we called the Low Road, along the shore by Lady Matheson's bathing shed.

It was to have provided what would have been regarded in these days as a broad highway across the moor to Arnish, but it got no further than the mouth of the Creed. Then the bubble burst, and Lewis wakened to the grim reality of life in the early twenties without a fairy godfather.

Lord Leverhulme was almost omnipresent in the life of a growing boy during the hectic years of his attempt to industrialise the island.

I remember the green floral arch with the inscription, "Welcome to Your Island Home" which greeted him on his first arrival as proprietor.

He had been to Lewis at least twice before. Once as a young man on a holiday cruise, and later as a prospective purchaser, spying out his kingdom incognito.

My mother's cousin, Roddie Smith, chemist, newsagent and several times provost, used to tell with great glee of his own first encounter with Lord Leverhulme. The millionaire haggled with him over the price of picture postcards of the town and castle!

On later visits Lord Leverhulme was greeted by the firing of rockets when the old "Sheila" came out of the darkness from the Minch, and the crowd which always assembled on the pier, waiting for their "morning" paper, two days old, at ten o'clock at night watched the masthead light appear for a moment in the dip of land near Prince Charlie's monument, vanish again behind the higher ground, and finally show clear and steady in the harbour mouth as she steamed round Goat Island for the quay.

I don't know whether there was any ceremony of greeting on these later arrivals, because I was always in my bed, although I was allowed to sit up and watch for the glow of the multicoloured rockets over the rooftops.

I would guess, however, that the brisk blocky figure, with the squarish face and pure white hair, would be standing on the bridge as the vessel docked, and would be quickly down the gangway to the waiting yellow Ford, shaking hands here and there, with some of his acquaintances in the town.

He must have had a remarkable memory for names and faces, and an intense interest in people, in spite of the many preoccupations of his business life.

I remember my father telling me how he was in Leverhulme's office at the Castle once to interview him, when an official came in to discuss the arrangements for the arrival of a new engineer — a relatively unimportant functionary — for his development plans in Lewis.

In those days there were no dining cars on Highland trains. It was necessary to arrange for a breakfast basket at Aviemore if one was not to starve on the long haul to Kyle from London.

Lord Leverhulme not only gave specific instructions that a basket of food should be ordered for the expected engineer, but knew enough of the man's family circumstances to add, "and remember a bottle of milk for the baby."

After my father-in-law emigrated, in the early twenties, Lord Leverhulme invited him, with my mother-in-law to dinner in New York.

Norman Stewart, a crofter's son from Back, had been a shopkeeper in Stornoway. Lord Leverhulme knew him as a bailie of the burgh and a supporter of his development plan. But, by the time he emigrated, Leverhulme had withdrawn from Lewis, he no longer needed to woo the local councillors, and, in any event, my father-in-law no longer had any official position or influence in the affairs of the town.

The invitation would never have been given if Lord Leverhulme had not had a

71

genius for friendship, regardless of rank or position, and a great affection for Lewis and its people.

It was many years later, in fact, shortly before my mother-in-law died that the family learned, quite by chance, that, in the course of that New York dinner, Lord Leverhulme had introduced his Lewis guests to a friend of his, dining at a nearby table — the legendary John D. Rockefeller.

I think, that, in turn, tells us a great deal about Lewis and its attitudes. The meeting with Rockefeller was not a secret, but on the other hand it was not paraded whenever the opportunity offered. A meeting with a fellow islander would have been more important.

There can be few places so genuinely and positively egalitarian as Lewis, in the sense that we value people for qualities of character, and not for the trappings of their office, their titles, or even their wealth.

The word "positively" in that paragraph is all important. There is a negative egalitarianism: a mean, envious and destructive knocking down, which is very different from what I have in mind. And much more prevalent!

25
The Hub of the Fishing Industry

Every Christmas during the Leverhulme regime many Stornoway families received a red tin box, rather like the Chancellor's famous despatch box, with a Viscount's coronet in gold on the top containing a wide assortment of the products of the Leverhulme Empire — brilliantine, soap, talcum powder, and scent.

Apart from the soap, the contents were not of much interest to our particular household, but the boxes were. They were ideal for storage, and survived for many years as repositories for my draughts and chessmen, and the family snapshots.

Leverhulme also sent out Christmas cards, probably to an even wider circle. One year a photograph of his Cheshire home, another year his home on Hampstead Heath. And, when he abandoned his attempt to develop Lewis and concentrated his interest on Harris, there was a Christmas card with a photograph of the first herring drifters to tie up at the new pier in Leverburgh — Obbe, renamed in his honour! — with the caption, "The Birth of Commerce."

Stillbirth it almost inevitably was in Leverburgh, because of the difficulties of the location, and even more because of his own untimely death.

But his earlier plan to develop Stornoway as "the hub of the fishing industry" — in his own phrase — was sound enough, if other people had been far enough sighted to share his vision.

He had great maps printed showing Stornoway as the natural centre of the North Atlantic fishing grounds, with the distances from the town marked off in circles at fifty mile intervals.

I had one on my office wall for many years, as a gentle hint to visitors that, though they might see it differently, Stornoway was to me the centre of the universe.

Leverhulme bought much of the house property in the town to demolish it. He wanted to make way for the Art Gallery he planned, and the Municipal Buildings, and the broad avenues sweeping right from the harbour front to the crest of Goathill.

He had a light railway plying from a quarry at the back of the hill on which the War Memorial now stands, down to the Braighe, to provide sand and shingle and quarry chips for his building programme. It was one of our great ambitions as boys to get a ride on the footplate of the train, and we sometimes did.

He built a canning factory and a freezing plant which never operated. When the crash finally came, my father bought a few lengths of steel piping from the freezing plant to make an aerial mast for our first radio.

Today you can carry a transistor, or even a miniature TV, in your waiscoat pocket, and dieve your neighbours with the noise it can produce. But at that time there were less than half a dozen radio sets in Lewis altogether. You required an outside aerial twenty feet high and fifty feet long to get worthwhile reception at all, and even then you had to listen closely with headphones. But what a thrill it was!

Part of the machinery from the abandoned canning factory was shipped to Spain, and some, I believe, to South Georgia. There was a rumour that, when the Herring Industry Board, a decade later, established a fish processing plant at Stornoway, the second-hand equipment they installed was some of Leverhulme's original plant coming home after a sojourn in the south Atlantic.

Even if the story is not true in fact, it can be regarded as a myth encapsulating a truth: the difference between Leverhulme's dream and the sort of treatment Lewis got at that time from government agencies.

Leverhulme built a score or so of semi-detached houses on Matheson Road for his higher executives, and a larger number at the top of Goathill for key workers. The first and only completed instalment of the re-created Stornoway. The new town at Arnish didn't begin at all.

I lived in one of the Leverhulme houses for many years. They were put on the market when his schemes were abandoned, and sold for considerably less than it cost to build them.

They were far ahead of Scottish municipal houses of that period in design, but they were built to an English specification. The walls were plastered on the hard, and there was no sarking on the roof. And that was not the best way to cope with Lewis rain.

The railway station for the passenger services of the island was to have been built where the Seaforth Hotel is today, and a cinema where the Comhairle have their headquarters. It was then a wilderness of wild irises.

In the same vicinity there was to have been a printing office to produce a daily newspaper.

My uncle, Duncan Grant, printed the "Gazette" at that time on his plant in Inverness. He came across to Stornoway to join in the discussions on the projected daily newspaper.

He was always a sanguine, dashing type. A good man in a crisis, but apt to be carried away by his own enthusiasm when things were going well. My father was more cautious, and, whether it was foresight, or premonition, or plain timidity, I do not know, but he held back from any rash commitment, which was wise in the light of subsequent events.

The cinema, the railway station and the printing office were never built. They were not even begun. The only permanent commercial result of Leverhulme's great plan for Lewis was the MacFisheries chain of fish shops, created to provide an outlet for the catch of the fleet of trawlers he planned to operate from Stornoway, but which, in the event, conferred no benefit on the town, even indirectly.

The name MacFisheries was an odd one for a Lancashire soap-maker to choose for his fish shops, but it gives a clue to the origin of the venture.

As for the printing office, it was more than twenty years later before the Gazette, still a very modest weekly, was first printed in Stornoway, on an antiquated flat-bed press, which I installed in an old naval canteen, re-erected in the garden of a rat infested house which served as an office.

To be precise, I should say that the plant was installed by Sam Longbotham. Although I was the editor and proprietor at that time, it was he who planned, and supervised, and carried through the Herculean task of dismantling the printing plant on the mainland, when one issue was completed, and re-erecting it in Stornoway in time to print the next.

There was no ferry service then so that the heavy plant had to be manhandled six times instead of twice, in and out of trains and steamers, and the whole thing had to be stripped almost to nuts and bolts to get it through the narrow entrance on Kenneth Street.

Without being asked, the staff worked throughout the night without a break rather than admit defeat. All except one, that is! The machineman from Glasgow was very drunk, which added an element of comedy to the night's proceedings, but rather impeded the work.

Many years later, when I was asked to address the St Andrew's Society in Winnipeg I was piped from the plane — much to my consternation. But the piper and I, as it turned out, were old friends.

He was Bob Fraser, one of that loyal band who brought the Gazette to Stornoway, now holding an important managerial post with a big Canadian printing firm.

26
Harry Lauder in SY

I knew Lord Leverhulme quite well by sight. Every Sunday, when he was in Lewis, he attended the morning service in Martin's Memorial, and sometimes read the lesson.

His voice had a gutteral, muffled quality which, no doubt, derived from the same cause as his deafness.

A bouncy little figure, with a grey silk topper, he used to sit in a pew near the front, in the middle of the church, where he had a hearing aid installed so that he could listen to the sermon despite his disability.

He offered to provide similar equipment for anyone in the congregation similarly afflicted.

A hearing aid installed in a church was a great novelty in those days, and might even have been looked at a little askance, although now we take microphones and amplifiers in church as a matter of course.

It was a lively time. There were always interesting guests at the Castle, or something stirring in the town, from a fete to a demonstration or a strike.

As a little boy in a sailor suit, I stood quite close to Harry Lauder when he opened the Stornoway Bowling Green. Harry offered to play an end with Leverhulme with the Castle as a stake. I cannot recall what, if anything, Harry proposed to put up as his own side of the wager. The canny Scot was not risking anything even in a joke!

I remembered the occasion well, but had forgotten my sailor suit until I opened some years ago an exhibition organised by the Lewis Amenity Society. In one of the photographs on view I spotted myself, standing beside my father as he sat on the edge of the platform, notebook in hand, recording Harry's wisecracks.

Not far away, in the same exhibition, was a home-made Lewis dress of the same period — a knitted skirt with a bodice made from an empty flour sack with the brand name still clearly visible.

The use of flour sacks in this way was commented on by Dr Porter, the M.O.H., in the report on social conditions in Lewis which I have already referred to. Nothing could remind one more eloquently of the poverty which prevailed in the early thirties, and the need for the work which Lord Leverhulme offered.

And nothing could underline more sharply the fact that it is not poverty which occasions crime or vandalism or rioting. These have their origin in attitudes of mind, not in the pay packet.

In the evening Harry Lauder sang at a concert in the old Picture House, or, as it was then, the new Picture House, on Keith Street, beside the Seminary. It was built to replace the earlier picture house at the other end of the street, where I had tried to get a job as a child shortly before it went on fire.

It was the only time I heard Harry Lauder sing, apart from recordings, which do not do him justice. It was a great occasion.

A few months later another star of the music hall, Charles Coburn, was a guest at the Castle and sang in the Picture House. He was then an old man, rather on his uppers. He had not, I think, come to Stornoway at the invitation of Lord Leverhulme, although he was given hospitality when he did arrive.

He sang for us, in a voice beginning to fail, the song that made him famous, "The Man that broke the bank at Monte Carlo."

I was familiar with the song before that, of course, having heard it sung with great verve by our own local Charles Coburn, Murdo "Gow".

Murdo was a great Stornoway character. He could be the subject of a book in himself. A ladies tailor he was very proper, almost effeminate, in his dealings with his clients, but for all that he had a salty tongue.

Stornowegians of my generation still tend to describe an unfortunate contretemps by a discreet reference to the calamity which overtook Murdo Gow's tea party, but without using the epigrammatic phrase with which he scandalised (or delighted!) his elegant guests.

My brother recalls an occasion when he saw Murdo hurrying along Bayhead with his week's wash in a basket. Suddenly a group of ladies from the Castle appeared on the horizon. They were clients of Murdo's.

It was clearly an embarrassing moment. Apart from the menial task he was engaged on, Murdo was not dressed for the company of the elite. In a moment he transformed himself. His jaw dropped, his head hung on the side, his mouth slobbered. He became the complete village idiot, and the ladies passed him by, noses in the air, without recognising him.

It was the same sort of quality he showed on the concert platform, but the transformation was very much in the other direction when he "walked along the Bois de Boulogne, with an independent air."

My father became quite friendly with some of the Castle guests. I remember him going to interview John Oxenham, then at the height of his rather evanescent fame as a novelist and poet. He gave my father autographed copies of some of his books, including "Bees in Amber," his collection of poems, which was refused by all the publishers he tried but sold several hundred thousand copies, when he published it at his own expense.

After his visit to Lewis he wrote a skit on Leverhulme's schemes called "Corner Island". It was a hilarious account of some London business men, and a Jewish financier, shipwrecked simultaneously on a remote Hebridean island.

They promptly got into competition with each other, trying to "corner" the island in the stock market sense. But, in the end of the day, they were, inevitably, taken to the cleaners by the Hebridean lighthouse keeper and his two comely daughters.

I don't think "Corner Island" added to Oxenham's reputation, and it seemed a little tasteless to accept Leverhulme's hospitality, and repay it in that way.

The closest friend my father made through Leverhulme's Castle guests was Alex Paul, Leverhulme's brother-in-law. He had been a journalist, I think he had been a leader writer on the old "Westminster Gazette". Certainly he and my father had a good deal in common, and kept up a correspondence until Paul's death.

He used to send my father wads of cuttings from the English newspapers of things he thought he might have missed. My father used them for dictation in his shorthand class at school, or when he gave me an occasional lesson at home.

So it happened that, as an odd by-product of Lord Leverhulme's schemes, a generation of Nicolsonian shorthand writers was brought up on the political commentaries of J. A. Spender and other Liberals of the old school.

I don't know whether they influenced anyone else, but they had a considerable effect on my own political views, and perhaps more on my literary style.

There was always something to discuss at meal times in those days.

Lord Leverhulme's arrival or departure. Some new and breath-taking development in his plans. A crisis which threatened to bring the whole thing to ruin.

A bit of tittle tattle about the latest ball or dinner party at the castle with a quiet snigger at the local worthy who drank the water in the finger bowls. I thought it hilarious because I knew I was expected to laugh, but, if the truth were told, I had no idea what finger bowls were.

Or a royal occasion when a naval vessel put into port with Prince George on board, and the unsuspecting Prince set the gossips of the town agog by dancing more than once with the rosy cheeked daughter of a very rough and ready butcher.

Or a real romance, when Lord Leverhulme's niece became engaged to a local medical student, "Dolly Doctor." After some years in Harley Street, they returned to Gisla, and then to Stornoway, where Lord Leverhulme's niece continued to live after her husband's death. A gracious lady, with a genuine love for the bleak northern town where she was somewhat cast ashore by the shipwreck of her uncle's plans.

27

The Best Paid Job in Town

Occasionally, during the Leverhulme regime, there was something quite outstanding like a fete in the Castle Grounds, with Tilting the Bucket, and other exotic sports we had never even heard of. At the same fete there was a battle scene from France, in a great marquee, with the British and German lines realistically set out, and more toy soldiers deployed than I thought existed in the world.

Then there was the mock heroic saga of the fire engine Lord Leverhulme presented to the town.

I have no recollection of it ever being used at a fire. I don't see how it could have been. It was steam driven, and, as one wag said, you would need three days notice of a fire, to get the boiler stoked.

On one occasion, however, it was used in Harris for a pumping job.

Lord Leverhulme's experts planned the journey with great care. They had relays of horses, and an army of men. They had blocks and tackle to haul the engine up the goat track at the Clisham which then served as the main road between Tarbert and Stornoway.

The journey took several days, and, when they wrote it up for the "Gazette," it read like an account of Hannibal crossing the Alps, complete with elephants.

When the job was done, and the experts had gone, and the Leverhulme regime was over, Stornoway got its engine back, very simply. A herring drifter was sent to collect it, at a suitable pier, at the right state of the tide, and it was in Stornoway in a matter of hours with no fuss.

In all the flurry of excitement over Leverhulme I think what interested us most was the installation of electric light at Lews Castle. It was the first electric light in Lewis, although an enterprising draper, Donald Macaulay, many years before I was born, had a poster in his window saying "Come and see our electric light."

In fact what he had installed was the first incandescent gas mantle to come to the island. Prior to that there were only the old fashioned flickering fanlights.

Although we were late in getting electricity, Stornoway was one of the first of the smaller towns in Scotland to have a gas plant. The city fathers used to boast that we had gas "before Greenock."

On one occasion the town was lit experimentally with gas distilled from peat. That was in the days when there was a Chemical Plant making paraffin from peat on the moor out by the Creed Lodge. It was a promising local industry brought to an abrupt end by the discovery of large deposits of natural oil in USA.

In charge of the electrical installation at the Castle was a typical Lewisman of his generation — Allan Maclean, a crofter's son from Brue, who had no formal training as an engineer, or for that matter as anything else, but who had roamed the world for many years picking up practical knowledge of men and machines as he went.

As a young man he worked his way across Canada from job to job. In Regina he fell in with another Lewisman.

"Well, Dan," he said to his new pal, "I'm going round every employment agency I can find until I know what's the best paid job in Regina. Then I'm going to apply for it."

"What if you don't know anything about it?" asked Dan.

"I don't know anything about any of them, so what does it matter?" said Allan. "Even if I can only hold it down for a couple of days, I'll know more about it than any other job in Canada, and I'll try again with another boss."

In that way Allan and Dan became "skinners" on the railway.

Their first job was to help round up the horses which had been loose all winter on the prairie, and get them yoked in teams. There was nothing the pair of them wouldn't have tackled on a boat, but horses were different. They had no idea where to begin.

Allan looked along the line of men until he saw one who seemed smart at his job. Then he let one of his own horses stray, and manoeuvred things so that he caught up with the wanderer alongside the man he had marked out.

With one eye on the expert and another on the horse, he made a fair shape at getting the harness on. He was then ready to go back for the rest of his team, and give a helping hand to Dan who was still wrestling helplessly with a tangle of leather.

From Regina he moved to British Columbia and became a miner. He was the only English speaker in a gang of Central Europeans, and the boss got into the habit of giving him the day's orders. The others resented this, until the day the boss made Allan his foreman.

Once he was vested with a little authority, the others were ready to lick his boots, a situation which embarrassed a man brought up in the egalitarian tradition of a Lewis crofting township.

"I was ashamed of the things they were prepared to do for me" he told me when I prised the story out of him, many years after the period when we frequented his engine shed to see how electricity was made.

We were standing together yarning, with our elbows on the wall of the Castle Grounds, beside the old boatman's house, which was then his home — a little grey tower which formed part of the wall, with a stone stairway down to the beach, where, in my childhood, there had been stepping stones across the muddy estuary to Bayhead Street.

I can still see him, in the sunshine, with his steel-rimmed spectacles, his puckered brow, and drooping grey moustache, which gave him rather a melancholy look, until his eye lit up at some fresh recollection, and his whole face opened in a smile.

When the Kaiser War broke out, he made his way back to Britain to report as a naval reservist. Not long afterwards he was Leading Seaman on a small vessel, the "Seamew", carrying out manoeuvres with a new anti-submarine device.

The "Seamew" was the first of the flotilla to complete the operation, a good fifteen seconds ahead of the next.

The Admiral who was watching the manoeuvres came on board to congratulate the captain, who very generously said a good deal of the credit must go to his acting Petty Officer.

80

The acting Petty Officer was sent for, and turned out to be a Leading Seaman, R.N.R., the only reservist in a flotilla of regulars.

"What was your occupation before the war?" asked the Admiral.

"A miner, sir," replied Allan. Later he admitted he had been a miner for only two years, and before that he had been a fisherman for fifteen.

"I must have you in Sheerness," said the Admiral.

Allan was taken on board HMS "Acteon", complimented on his work before the ship's company, and promoted Petty Officer, first class.

When I coaxed the story out of him, he was neither fisherman, miner, skinner, crofter, navyman or electrical engineer. He was a Harris Tweed weaver, and I had gone to consult him about some complicated problem which had blown up in the weavers' union, in which he then played a leading part.

Allan had been dead for many years before I learned from my brother, Eric, that he had acquired his knowledge of electricity from a set of books he picked up in America. They were called "Hawkins' Electrical Guide." Eric said they looked like Bibles with black morocco leather covers, and gilt edges. The information was set out in the form of questions and answers with illustrations of quite remarkable clarity.

Eric was so impressed he got a set for himself. But, quite apart from the books, he spent hours, even days, with Allan in his little shed behind the Castle, discussing his work, against a background of chugging engines, and a pervasive smell of acid from the accumulators and carboys.

28
It was all in the Tea Leaves

I don't know where my brother got the instinct for engines which led him to spend so much time with Allan Maclean, in the generating room at the Castle, but he had it almost from childhood.

I remember my father telling of the mixture of chagrin and pleasure he felt on one occasion when he was struggling unsuccessfully to start the engine of his motor bicycle. He was on the point of giving up in exasperation when Eric, little more than a child, leaned across from the sidecar and told him what to do.

Once Eric's instinct for engines saved his life.

With a group of his pals, he was on board the "Children's Trust" — an ironical name as it turned out.

The "Children's Trust" was a fishing boat, owned by Murdo MacLean, Stephen's father, who had the Lewisman's versatility. At different times in his career he was a clerk with the old Parochial Board, the manager of a steamboat company, a tweed merchant, a travel agent, consul for the Finnish government, and, when all else seemed to have failed him because of a change in the pattern of trade, — a banker.

He was a busy, rather aggressive, little man who had some enemies, but, when Lord Leverhulme's schemes collapsed, he did the island a notable service of which I will have something to say later.

It must have been towards the end of the Kaiser War he made his short adventure into the fish trade.

The engine of the "Children's Trust", as in so many fishing boats of the period had a system of hot bulb ignition, which meant that it had to be started up with blow lamps.

Eric was in the engine room with the others when the blow lamps were lit and put in their brackets, but he knew from the sound they were making that something was wrong.

He tried to get up on deck but his way was barred. Bob Scott, a local engineer, was standing on the ladder talking to someone on the quay. His head and shoulders were thrust through the hatch and he was unaware of what was happening below. The conversation, Eric felt, lasted an eternity.

As soon as it was over and Bob Scott came off the ladder, Eric dashed up it. As he reached the deck there was an explosion, and the vessel caught fire.

There was a scramble for the ladder. Several of the boys were scorched, some of them badly. One, Conrad Ross, the son of a local solicitor, was trapped below and burned to death.

However efficient, or even callous, a reporter on a local newspaper may be, he can never be quite indifferent to the news he records. He is himself, in a very real sense, part of it.

The fire, and the fatal accident inquiry which followed, were "copy" for my father. But his involvement in the night long search for Connie Ross was personal and harrowing, as the family and friends tried to pretend to themselves that there was still a chance that he had escaped alive, but was too frightened to come home.

Many years later my mother told me part of the story which was not reported at the time, and which she spoke of with reluctance even then.

On the afternoon of the fire, she was at a tea party in Mrs Ross's. The party had been arranged to introduce to some of the ladies of the town a new Matron, Nurse Galbraith, who had just come to Lewis Hospital.

In the course of the party, it emerged that Nurse Galbraith read teacups. She was pressed to do so. She didn't know the ladies present and they thought it would be a good test of her skill.

Looking into my mother's cup she told her that she saw her meeting someone at a boat. She had gone to the boat with great trepidation but the meeting made her very happy.

She told Mrs MacLean that she saw a strange boat in her cup without mast or funnel. She also told her she would receive some money in unusual circumstances.

The strange boat appeared again in Mrs Ross's cup with tears and weeping. She, too, was to receive money which she did not want.

While the cup reading was still in progress, there was a commotion outside. Then someone burst in to tell them the "Children's Trust" was on fire.

Almost every woman present at the party, except Nurse Galbraith, had a son on board it that day. They were to have been taken out for a sail.

Douglas Ross came running in, badly burned about the neck. Peter MacLean arrived shortly afterwards, also slightly burned. No one had any idea what had happened to Conrad Ross or Eric.

My mother raced to the pier. There she found Eric, standing among the crowd, unhurt, watching the attempts being made to fight the fire.

It was not until next day, when the "Children's Trust" was a burnt-out shell, beached on the far side of the harbour, below the Castle wall, without mast or funnel, that the charred remains of Conrad Ross were found.

Rightly or wrongly, my mother assumed that the references to money in Nurse Galbraith's cup-reading related to insurance claims.

So far as I know my mother was completely free from superstition, or from any belief in "second sight" but that experience troubled her.

The only member of the family who ever claimed to have second sight, so far as I know, was born in Sydney, Australia, just as far from Highland superstition as one can get.

Anna Irwin, a niece of Willie Pope of the tarred bottoms, told me once that when Willie's ship was torpedoed in the Second World War, she had a strange experience.

The first report said that there had been no survivors, and she decided to hurry back to Sydney from the small town where she was living, to be with her mother, whom she knew would be distressed.

She had to catch a very early train but she did get some sleep. In the course of it she dreamed vividly that her uncle had been rescued and landed in Nova Scotia.

When she got to Sydney she told her mother not to worry, Willie was all right.

The minister reproved her for this, saying it was cruel to build up false hopes. But Anna persisted. "It's all right," she said. "I know".

As it happened she did.

Whether my grandfather was right when he thought he had a brush with the supernatural is something that can never be proved or disproved.

His brother-in-law, John Smith was drowned at sea. His vessel the "Raven" went down with all hands.

Some years later, my grandfather, crossing the Bay of Biscay, dreamt that John Smith rose from the sea, and said to him, "Tell Tarmod Ruadh it was no fault of mine."

The dream was so vivid my grandfather was convinced he had sailed over the spot where the "Raven" went down.

John Smith was married to a sister of my grandmother. It was in his home the family sheltered when the roof blew off my grannie's house. Roddie Smith, a leading figure in the public life of the town for many years, was John Smith's son. Sandy Matheson, the convener of the Comhairle, is John Smith's great grandson.

Tarmod Ruadh who owned the "Raven" was Norman Maciver, the banker, one of the two Trustees of the Ness Disaster Fund who refused to take part in the attempt to whitewash Donald Munro's activities as treasurer.

If I mistake not, it was a daughter of his who was known to my generation of Stornowegians as "Little Auntie." She was a petite, aristocratic, almost birdlike lady, who surprisingly, had a large family of exceptionally tall, handsome, elegant daughters.

Malcolm Maclean, the baker, is her grandson.

29
Spooks and the Hydro Board

It was only once I had an experience even remotely resembling my mother's tea party on the day the "Children's Trust" caught fire.

I dreamt one night that I met David Tolmie, then a prominent figure in the Harris Tweed industry, in the Post Office. He was all in black, and muffled to the throat, which was most unusual for one of the best dressed men in town. But it was his face which caught my attention. It was a hideous, bloated purple.

"I'm glad to see you out again," I said to him in the dream, a little hesitantly, knowing that he had been indisposed for some days.

"It's not good like that," he replied. "Did you not know that I was going away?"

I wakened then, and the dream was still so vivid I looked at my watch and took a note of the time. It was 7.45. When I went down town, I learned that David Tolmie had died that morning.

There is a simple explanation of my dream. The previous day I had called on David's brother, Willie John Tolmie, in his chemist's shop, to ask how David was because I knew he had been laid up.

Willie John was clearly worried. He told me that he was afraid his brother was worse than even the doctor seemed to realise.

It was just a coincidence that the dream wakened me so close to the time of his death. It was not far from my usual time for wakening anyway.

Some years ago an American mathematician tried to demonstrate that instances of second sight (so called) or telepathy are pure chance and can be explained statistically.

We all have fancies at times, he argued, about people who are distant from us. We remember the occasions when our fancy proves to be true, or an approximation to the truth. We forget the times when our fancies are wildly wrong.

If we could add up all the right guesses, and all the wrong guesses, we would find, said the American, that the number of right guesses was an infinitesimal part of the total, and no more than could be accounted for by random chance.

I wonder!

One of the most circumstantial accounts of an encounter with the supernatural I ever had came from a hard headed engineer. Not the sort of man one would have thought addicted to idle fancies. He was an islander, however, from Islay, I think, so it may have been in his blood.

I forget what the occasion of our meeting was, but I was sitting in the upstairs lounge of the County Hotel, with Sir Edward MacColl of the North of Scotland Hydro Electric Board. Somehow the conversation came round to the supernatural and Sir Edward said, quite simply, and flatly, that his home in Clydebank had been haunted.

When I asked him about it, he said the house had been built by an eccentric

85

architect named Macleod. The man he built it for did not like it, and sold it cheaply to the architect himself to get rid of it.

Not long afterwards Macleod, the architect, died in the house, and the MacColl's bought it.

Sir Edward was in Belgium when the family moved in. But, when he returned, he found them in a state of some excitement. All the bells in the house were jangling continuously.

"Ah", said Sir Edward, "we must have rats." But there were no rats, and mysterious noises continued even after the old fashioned bell-pulls had been removed.

Then one day, as they sat at lunch, they saw a man walk up towards the front door. They waited for him to ring, or knock. But he did neither. In fact, no one knocked, or entered, or walked away again.

They became quite familiar, he said, with this mysterious person who was seen, or heard, approaching the house but never got there. They identified him with the architect and called him Macleod.

Sometimes, he said, when one of the family was ready to go out they would hear Macleod approaching the door, but however quickly it was opened there was no one there, although there could not possibly have been time for anyone to hide.

Sir Edward concluded the story by saying that the house was destroyed in the Clydebank blitz. It was then in process of being rebuilt. He wondered whether it would still be haunted, or whether the Nazi bombs had exorcised the ghost.

I never found out. Sir Edward died not very long after our conversation, and I never met him again.

But either he believed the story implicitly, and accepted a haunted house as completely natural, or else he was an incomparable raconteur, perpetrating the leg pull of a lifetime.

The war, of course, was a fruitful time for stories of the supernatural, some of them very circumstantial, but it was always difficult to know how much they owed to our Lewis gift for making a good story better as we pass it on.

It was a well-known Stornowegian who once said to me in some exasperation, "Half the lies you hear in this town aren't true."

One day during the war — the Second World War — Ian Maclean, one of my closest friends, but no relation of Stephen, told me of a conversation he had with a sailor from a rural village.

The sailor told him that, around 1933, he had been in the R.N.R. His kit was hanging in a wardrobe at home.

His mother complained that she heard a strange knocking coming from the wardrobe, but she could find no explanation. although she searched it several times.

She finally came to the conclusion that the noise was coming from her son's uniform, and shifted it to a chest in an outhouse. The knocking stopped.

This convinced her that the knocking was an evil omen, associated with the uniform. She pled with her son to leave the RNR. She was so distressed he did not rejoin when his engagement was up.

The incident was completely forgotten, but, when war broke out, a younger brother joined the navy. Once when he was home on leave Ian's informant gave him the old uniform, together with a lanyard and a knife.

When the brother returned to his depot wearing the uniform he was transferred to another ship. An hour after he joined it, the ship was blown up.

The story as I got it was very circumstantial. It even included the name of the village and the name of the ship. I did not use the story, nor check it out. That, I felt, would merely have distressed a mother already prostrate with grief.

The effect of the story, however, is offset by the fact that at least two other Lewismen were lost on the same ship. They, too, had been drafted on board at the last minute to fill vacancies, but there had been no premonition of disaster so far as I am aware.

Some so called hauntings, of course, are readily explicable. My grandfather used to tell of a Lewis seaman who had an encounter with the devil in a South American port.

He had been put ashore suffering from yellow fever. A fellow townsman whose unamiable disposition is recorded in his nickname — George the Poison — was convalescent in a neighbouring bed.

He did not reveal his identity, but in the middle of the night began to torment his acquaintance, by muttering in Gaelic, intimate details of his past life, with threat of the retribution which was in store for him when the devil got him.

There was a story current in my youth about a Stornoway landlady angling to marry a rather simple minded lodger, who professed to hear spiritual voices from time to time.

Taking advantage of the situation, she hid under his bed one night, and muttered repeatedly in the darkness, "Pos Kate! Pos Kate!"

They were married, and "Pos Kate!" was a current expression in Stornoway in my youth.

30
When the King was Framed

Although I saw Lord Leverhulme on many occasions, it was only once that I spoke to him, and then very diffidently. I was probably twelve at the time, or just entering my teens. Certainly young enough and old enough, to be a little overawed by the occasion.

We had not, in my generation, attained the emancipated familiarity with our seniors which later enabled a young Stornowegian, the son of a minister, to rebuke a visiting Moderator at table with the comment, "Och, man, you're just a blether".

Or to ask the Right Reverend Dr Watt, "Are you a brother of Dr Who?"

We had just moved into one of the houses built by Leverhulme on Matheson Road, saying farewell for good, and with some relief, to Mrs Maclennan and her hens.

The new house was much smaller than the old one. My mother, in fact, threatened to call it the "Matchbox," and some of her friends, taking her at her word, surprised the postman by using that as if it were the real name.

Although it seemed small by the standards one applied to houses, in the town at least, in the early twenties, it would probably be considered quite reasonable today.

It had two living rooms as well as the kitchen. There were four bedrooms, although one was very small. And there were toilets both upstairs and down. Which suggests that we were still living in an era when a professional man was expected to have a maid.

Despite the smaller size, it was a great improvement on the Lewis Street house. We had gas light for one thing. No more oil lamps, or candles dripping blobs of grease across the carpet as we carried them carelessly to bed.

It even had hot water from a boiler behind the living room fire. That was luxury indeed in Lewis in the early twenties, when the great majority of the population were still in thatched houses, without any running water at all. Some without even a chimney to release the smoke.

We accept the living standards of the present day as if they were no more than we were entitled to, and had been fully earned by our own endeavours.

People of my generation, especially those from rural villages, know how fortuitous, in a sense, these things are, and how little they are related to the individual's endeavours, or his worth, on any standard of assessment we care to apply.

When one compares the living standards which exist today with those which existed in rural Lewis half a century ago, or with those which still exist over the greater part of the inhabited globe, one wonders whether we are not living in a revolutionary situation with the ordinary working man in the Western world, dissatisfied though he may be with his pay packet, cast in the role of the French aristocrat of 1789. It's a sombre thought!

There was one minor, but troublesome, defect in the construction of the new house, of which we did not become aware at once. There was a stone slightly out of place in the chimney, forming a ledge where soot gathered.

The result was that, long before the chimney should have needed cleaning, we had a spectacular chimney fire.

It happened in the middle of the morning, when we were having the room papered for the first time. The walls had originally been distempered to give the plaster time to dry out properly.

It was one of the funniest situations I have ever been involved in — like something out of the Marx brothers, or, perhaps, Laurel and Hardy.

My mother was rushing to and fro with buckets of blazing soot. The room was filled with smoke. It looked as if the whole place might go up at any moment. Eric and I were dashing here and there, more busy than helpful.

In the midst of it all, taciturn, slow-moving Dan Mackay, the painter, apparently oblivious of all that was happening around him, was trying to get my mother to chose a border for the room.

Sample book in hand, he tried repeatedly to waylay her as she dashed by with her buckets of soot. He seemed strangely puzzled that she paid so little attention to the decoration of her house.

It was on a Sunday afternoon Lord Leverhulme came to call. He had been invited to afternoon tea to give him an opportunity of seeing one of his new houses, once it had been furnished and made into a home.

He probably organised the invitation himself. It was more in keeping with Lord Leverhulme's character to want to see for himself, than it was in keeping with my father's to invite someone to the house from outwith his own immediate circle of friends.

Eric and I were not permitted to be present at the tea. We were packed off to my grannie's in Newton. But we were allowed to stay until Lord Leverhulme arrived, and were briefly introduced to him.

I think it must have been on that occasion that Lord Leverhulme told my father of the tour of inspection he had made of his model town, Port Sunlight, some years before.

In one of the houses he was surprised to find that the toilet seat was missing. How could anything have got broken in so short a time?

When he asked about it, he was proudly shown the seat, removed from its moorings, and hanging on the wall, to frame a picture of the King.

I told the story of my meeting with Lord Leverhulme to the present holder of the title when he came to Stornoway to take part in Magnus Magnusson's BBC programme on the attempt by his grandfather to industrialise Lewis.

When, a short time later, the two of us were placed before the cameras, (down on the beach at Holm, for some odd reason,) Lord Leverhulme startled me by opening the discussion with the remark, "I understand you knew my grandfather well."

The man who addressed the remark to me was probably in his fifties, and looked a good deal more, because he seems to have inherited his grandfather's deafness. It was the only time in my life I have been made to feel like Methuselah.

The last time I saw Lord Leverhulme — the original Lord Leverhulme — was when he unveiled the Lewis War Memorial to which he had been a very generous contributor.

He had left Lewis for good by then, but despite the shipwreck of his schemes, he was still interested in the island, and certainly bore us no ill will.

I was present at the ceremony as a Boy Scout, and, being one of the smallest in the troop I was near the front with a good view of everything.

I had a fair understanding of the nature and solemnity of the ocassion, but saw things very much from a child's point of view.

The principal function of the War Memorial up to that time, so far as I was concerned, was as a playground. During the construction we used to go out from time to time to inspect progress of what was to us a wonderful erection.

On one occasion, four of us, unobserved by the watchman, sneaked in and climbed up the successive ladders and platforms to the top of the tower. It was a great adventure, until we realised that we had been spotted. Then there was a mad scramble to escape.

Stephen Maclean, and Willie Gow, whose father was one of Lord Leverhulme's engineers, got clean away.

Hugh Cullum and I were trapped at first floor level. The watchman had removed the ladder.

I don't know how long we were marooned but it seemed like an eternity. But when he had had his fun, the watchman let us go with nothing more serious than a perfunctory kick on the bottom.

Although familiar with the Memorial and its function, it was some years later before I understood the true significance of the brass plaques with the names of the fallen, and of those who had lost their lives in the Iolaire disaster, not only in terms of individual grief for the families directly affected, but in social implications for the life and development of the whole community.

31
A Freudian Carapace

I was only eight when the "Iolaire" was lost, but I well remember being wakened by my father that New Year's morning. I don't know how much he told us, or was able to tell us, then, but we knew, at least, that something terrible had happened.

It was the family custom to gather on Xmas day in my uncle's manse to eat a turkey, and, on New Year's Day, in my grannie's to eat a goose, both sent home from Durham by my uncle Willie.

These were two big days in my calendar as a youngster, although Christmas was not much observed in Lewis at that time. In my childhood I never saw a Christmas tree, in fact the Christmas holidays (so called) sometimes did not begin until Christmas had passed, so that we went to school on Christmas morning.

On New Year's Day, of course, we were always free. I have a feeling that there was sometimes a concert in the evening. I may be confusing different occasions in my memory, but I have a recollection of looking with wonder at the red, or yellow, or blue tickets of admission which my parents had. Feeling quite grown up and excited when they set off, and we were left in the care of my granny, and my aunts, until their return, long after any normal bedtime, when we would walk home through the dark — no taxis then! — and I would snuggle inside my father's coat for warmth, peeping out between the lower buttons like a rabbit taking a wary look from its burrow.

New Year's Day 1919 was different. Our play was muted. It was more like a Sunday than a holiday in mood. My father came in only for odd moments now and then. In spite of his massive frame and ruddy, almost always smiling face, he was like the death's head at a feast. Each fleeting visit brought a new tale of horror to distress the assembled family.

He was the only reporter on the island, handling the biggest story of his life, and doing it with such professional competence that a senior reporter from the "Times" travelling to Stornoway to cover the disaster, was recalled at Inverness, because there was nothing left for him to do.

But my father was also a member of the community, stunned and shocked and troubled by the greatest tragedy that had ever befallen it.

Dostoevsky writes of "the strange feeling of self-satisfaction" which "can always be observed, even in near relatives, in the case of some sudden misfortune, and which all men, without exception, experience, however sincere their concern and sympathy."

No doubt my father was protected by this Freudian carapace, and buoyed up for a time by the exhilaration which every journalist feels when covering great events, but he was also sensitive to other peoples' sorrows, and was often troubled by the knowledge that the misfortunes of his friends brought grist to his mill.

The Iolaire disaster and its impact on himself and the community was one of the

91

last things he discussed with me, when he was on his death bed, a dozen years later.

We gathered the facts of the disaster from him in snippets as the day wore on, and, even when the secret Admiralty papers were opened to inspection half a century after the event, there was little to add to what he had pieced together in the first few hours.

It began with a familiar situation — chaos at Kyle of Lochalsh because neither the War Office nor the Admiralty had made adequate provision for the number of servicemen coming home on leave.

Exactly the same had happened some seventeen years earlier when the Lewis soldiers came home from the Boer War. On that occasion there was a protest at the scandal, but no disaster. In 1919 it was different.

More than fifty men were stranded overnight at Kyle on the 30th of December with no provision made for them. The mail steamer "Sheila" had not been able to accommodate all who tried to get aboard.

The next day — New Year's Eve — five hundred more were disgorged at Kyle from jam-packed trains.

It was then the authorities took a hasty, and as it proved, a fatal decision. They sent the parent ship of the Stornoway naval base, H.M. Yacht "Iolaire," to Kyle to take the overflow.

The soldiers and civilians were assigned to the regular mail steamer, the "Sheila". Two hundred and sixty naval ratings were assigned to the "Iolaire".

Captain Cameron of the "Sheila" knew the Minch like the back of his hand. But the "Iolaire" had never previously entered Stornoway harbour in the dark.

The passengers on the "Iolaire" that night included many boys in their teens coming home on their first leave since enlistment. There were also veterans who had been at sea since August 1914, looking forward to their first reunion with their wives.

Many met schoolmates they had not seen since they were mobilised together. Some of the older men met cousins, or even brothers, they had left behind as pupils in the village school.

Two hours steaming from Stornoway the New Year was welcomed in time honoured fashion. All were in high spirits. Gaelic songs were sung. And there was talk of the welcome awaiting them round the blazing peat fires of a hundred Lewis villages.

When Arnish Light drew near, they began to gather their kit. In a few minutes they would be tied up at the familiar wharf from which they had set out on what many of them, at the time, had regarded as a high adventure.

Suddenly there was a crash. The ship heeled to starboard. Waves broke over her. Fifty or sixty men jumped into the sea and attempted to swim ashore. All of them were drowned.

No orders were heard from the bridge, but one of the "passengers" found rockets and fired them.

The rockets lit up the landscape and they saw the shore. It was only a dozen yards from the stern, but between was an angry cauldron of surf in which no one could live.

Then, as the ship settled, she swung broadside to the shore, breaking the force of the sea amidships. A few men swam to safety, among them John F. MacLeod from Port of Ness, who took a life line with him, by which a hawser was pulled ashore.

Thirty or forty followed along the hawser. Altogether seventy five escaped from the stricken ship.

No one will ever know how many perished because no passenger list was kept at Kyle, but the official inquiry set the tally at two hundred and five.

The relatives of some of those who perished were gathered on the pier to meet them. Almost within sight of the shipwreck, yet unaware of it.

Some of the townsfolk were also astir, first footing in the traditional New Year style, but most were abed having heard the ship's sirens in the harbour usher in the first New Year of peace.

Many of them had attended the traditional Watch Night services in the various churches, which in those days attracted large attendances, thanking God that the horror of war had been lifted from their lives.

32
A Fragment of The Rail

The first to learn of the "Iolaire" disaster were the Anderson Youngs at Stoneyfield farmhouse.

About three o'clock in the morning one of the survivors in a dazed condition stumbled into the farmhouse, and roused the inmates. He had no idea where he was.

Mrs Young and her maids were quickly alerted and began to prepare for further survivors. They arrived in little groups, attracted by the lights now showing from the farmhouse windows.

As the accommodation in the farmhouse rapidly filled up, those who were able to set off for Stornoway, to rouse their friends and relatives in town.

The last time I was speaking to my cousin, Ancrise Ross, she recalled how she had been wakened that morning, early, by someone knocking at the door. It was a friend from Carloway, George Morrison, son of the Rev. Neil M. Morrison, a survivor, seeking shelter and a change of clothes.

A short time later a neighbour, Mrs Macaskill, arrived to ask if he had any information about her son, Jackie, who she believed had also been on board. Jackie Macaskill was among those lost.

Soon the town was ringing with news of the disaster, and large numbers of people made their way to Holm.

Sandwick Beach was strewn with wreckage, and here and there a body which was lifted above the tide mark, clear of the sea.

It was dark when the first of the townsfolk reached the scene. The "Iolaire" had already disappeared, all but the masts, and one of them was broken.

Clinging precariously to the top of the unbroken mast was a young lad from Ness, Donald Morrison of Knockaird. Within speaking distance of the shore, but beyond help, because of the high sea running.

Two men who had been with him on the mast had grown numb, and fallen into the sea. His own strength was ebbing as the anguished spectators watched and waited.

As daylight broke, the wind began to moderate, and sometime between nine and ten in the morning, more than seven hours after the wreck, oil was poured on the sea, and a small boat was able to approach the "Iolaire" and take him off.

Rather ironically the only time I ever met Donald Morrison was shortly after the outbreak of the Second World War, when the Lewis naval reservists were again engaged in their country's defence.

The irony derived from the fact that we met in Stornoway Sheriff Court when he was giving evidence against a poaching trawler.

As soon as war broke out, the Fishery protection vessels were removed to other duties, and the few fisherman who remained in the villages which manned the naval reserve were at the mercy of any trawler which cared to come in.

Morrison had identified a trawler with binoculars from the shore, and the offender was brought to book. But that had little effect on the general depredation.

Ness suffered heavily in the Iolaire disaster. Altogether 23 Nessmen were lost. Point also suffered heavily. Between Holm and Tiumpan there were forty casualties. Between Back and Tolsta there were twenty. More than twenty between Barvas and Shawbost. Another twenty from the villages of North Lochs. And six from the tiny village of Crowlista in Uig.

For days after the disaster I was not allowed out alone, in case I wandered down to the temporary mortuary established at the Naval Barracks, because the town mortuary on Cromwell Street Quay was quite inadequate for such a need, or to the beach at Holm itself where the grim work of recovering the dead was still going on.

My brother, being older, had more freedom. He saw for himself the horror of it all and brought back from the beach a broken fragment of the "Iolaire's" handrail, which I still have.

Although I was shielded from the disaster, I did not escape it. Perhaps I felt it more keenly, just because I had been kept away. I lived through these days in imagination instead of having my childish curiosity slaked by the stark reality.

It was the first event in my life which really got home to me. I had no relatives, or friends, or even close acquaintances, on board the "Iolaire", but I still cannot speak of it, or even think of it, without being close to tears, as I have often been when I have read again my father's description of the scene, written hastily a few hours after it happened.

"After leaving the road as it turns into Holm Farm", he wrote, "a walk of a few hundred yards brought one to the greensward overlooking the wreck. There were gathered no idle sightseers, for all had come in quest of the remains of relatives.

"On the grass had been laid out the bodies that had been recovered from the sea, and below the crews of eight rowboats proceeded in silence with their work of dragging round the wreck.

"At very short intervals the grappling irons brought another and another of the bodies to the surface, and the crews proceeded with them to the ledge where they were being landed. Here they were placed on stretchers, and slowly and laboriously the bearers clambered up with them to be laid out reverently on the grassland above.

"Scarce a word was spoken, and the eyes of strong men filled with tears as the wan faces were scrutinised with mingled hope and fear of identification."

No one knew who precisely had been on board and who had not. Sometimes a crofter doing a neighbourly service for some widow with no one to send, came on his own son, or nephew, unexpectedly, among the dead.

"The remains as they were recovered were brought to a temporary mortuary at the Naval Barracks, where relatives of the missing men, from all parts of the island gathered.

"As the bodies were identified, they were handed over to the friends and a little procession of carts, in groups of two or three, each with its coffin, passed through the Barrack gates on their way to some mourning village for interment."

It was sometimes nightfall before the carts reached home with the remains of those for whom a dram and a kiss and a Gaelic blessing had been prepared.

I remember once being given a vivid description, long after the event, by an elderly lady of a burial which took place, perforce, at night by the light of lanterns.

The memory of that funeral, which I did not see, has remained with me. It seems symbolic of an event which broke all the norms, even for a community inured to disaster at sea.

An event which the community accepted with resignation and stoicism but which probably bit more deeply into the soul because of that very fact.

33
Salvation Tethered to Damnation

I cannot recall Anderson Young, in whose farm the first survivors from the "Iolaire" found refuge. I must have known him, but I can call up no picture in my mind. Yet he figures quite prominently in my reminiscences of Lewis, even if it is in a rather shadowy way.

He, or it may have been his father, figures in some of the stories I have heard from older friends.

The Youngs were not so much farmers as salmon fishers. In my childhood there was a small sheet of water known as Young's Pond between Seaforth Road and Knockgarry, which was then the Parish Kirk Manse.

Young's Pond, I think was artificial. Its function was to provide ice to preserve the salmon on their way to market.

At the end of the last house on the road from Newton down to Sandwick beach there was a very solidly constructed shed which we knew as Young's ice house. There were no windows, as I recall, and the door faced north. I think it is more by logical (or illogical) deduction, rather than from precise information, I came to believe that it was used to store ice from the winter for summer needs.

Certainly Young's Pond seems to have frozen very readily. My mother once described for me how she and her contemporaries spent their winter nights skating there by the light of kerosene flares set round about on upturned barrels.

It must have been a particularly hard winter, at least I gathered the impression that the skating went on for a very long time. That, of course, may have been an illusion in my mother's mind, like the long summers of unbroken sunshine I remember from my own childhood. It never rained when I was a boy!

Young (father, son or it may be grandfather) had the reputation of being a practical joker, and a wag. I think it was he who passed a comment about the spire of Martin's Memorial which became proverbial in the town.

At one point during the construction of the spire the scaffolding or cranes, straddled the street, and had to be anchored to the beer store of the Imperial Hotel, which later became the Girls' Hostel.

"Salvation tethered to damnation!" said Young.

Colin Scott Mackenzie, the father, and predecessor, of the present Procurator Fiscal, once told me a story about "old Young" as he called him.

Young had occasion to divert the Barvas River in connection with his salmon fishing operations.

He was working away with Ross, his gamekeeper, when they came on a skeleton. They presumed it had been washed up by the tide at some time or another, and reburied it.

They were conscious, however, that they had been observed by a man who was not on particularly good terms with Young, and who promptly complained to the police.

Next day Young took Ross, from whom the story came, down to the machair. They sat there for some time enjoying the sun, while Young kept an eye on the main road from town.

Ross was puzzled. Then he saw a gig approaching. Young took up his telescope and trained it on the gig. Chuckling merrily, he handed the telescope to Ross.

In the gig were the Procurator Fiscal from Stornoway, and the Superintendent of Police. They were met by the policeman from Barvas, and carried on down towards Arnol.

There they were met by Young's enemy, Alastair Ruadh, and they all proceeded down the Barvas River to the place where the skeleton had been unearthed.

Young and Ross watched through the telescope while Alastair Ruadh dug vigorously, protesting all the time that the bones of his ancestors had been desecrated. Then he bent and picked something up. The others stepped back, laughing heartily.

He had in his hand a ram's head, complete with horns.

Alastair Ruadh guessed what had happened, and shook his fist in the direction of Young's house.

The official party then set off themselves towards Young's house, presumably to inquire into the discovery of the skeleton and the substitution of the ram's head.

At that point Ross heard Young mutter, "Damn it all. I forgot to set the bridge!"

He had apparently anticipated that the party would cross the river towards his house by a little wooden footbridge, and had intended to set a stone under one corner in the hope of tipping them into the river.

Perhaps it was as well for him he forgot.

The most celebrated incident with which the Youngs were connected was the great whale hunt of 1867, when over a hundred whales came into Stornoway harbour, and were driven up Bayhead, until they stranded themselves on the beach.

The entry of the whales into the harbour was fortuitous. The stranding was deliberate.

The whales were first sighted when Young went out to inspect his salmon nets at the mouth of the Creed.

As soon as the news got around every boat that would float was hurriedly pushed out. Everything that could be used to splash the water and scare the whales was pressed into service.

A school of whales was a real windfall in those days. The oil alone was of great value. And the scenes of activity in the Inner Harbour when the whales were being cut up were spoken of in Stornoway for many years.

When I heard the story first, fifty years after the event, it was still referred to as if it had happened yesterday.

My uncle Roddie saw the whale hunt as a boy of seven. He was wakened by his mother with the shout, "The town has been taken by whales." He gave me a vivid account of it when he was in his nineties, naming many of the worthies who had been active in the chase and in the kill.

The story was most effectively kept alive in a poem by James Disher who might be described, without disrespect, as the MacGonagle of Lewis.

I used to be able to recite great swatches of it. But all I remember now is a reference to Young's astonishment when he found "Six score whales and mair a-reiving at his nets, man."

Whale hunts were relatively common in the islands last century, although the Stornoway whale hunt seems to have been outstanding for the size of the kill.

The Rev. Hely Hutchison, a sportsman who came regularly to Lewis for more than twenty years, describes, in his reminiscences, a whale hunt in Loch Seaforth.

The whales were first sighted off East Loch Tarbert. The Harrismen followed them north trying to turn them into Loch Seaforth.

When they were sighted at Loch Seaforth all the fishermen in the area joined in the hunt, under the direction of Murdo Macaulay, who seems to have been a gamekeeper, possibly at Aline.

The whales were gently shepherded up the loch towards Airidhbhruaich, but they halted at the Narrows, apparently unwilling to proceed against the strong current on the ebb tide. A little patience, however, and they would have been secured when the tide turned.

But at that time the hunters were reinforced (disastrously) by what Hutchison describes as "one of the dirtiest, crankiest tubs of a boat" he had ever seen with less grip of the water than a Thames "punch bowl". He could not imagine how it ever came round from Tarbert in safety.

"The crew consisted of three of the ugliest, noisiest, most ill-conditioned-looking viragoes of women...perched up in their boat like so many witches wanting their broomsticks. One of them sat upon a turf creel in the bows, knitting for bare life...

"Their voices", he said, "set your teeth on edge, and their laughter made you try and stop your ears. It was evident that they were bent on mischief, and that to maintain discipline with these three Gorgons was impossible."

The "triumvirate of demons" he concludes, "deaf to all entreaties," went in with a whoop, at the wrong moment, and scared the whales, which turned tail, and fled for the sea and safety.

That, I think, tells us a little about whales, nothing about Harris, and a good deal about the Rev Hely Hutchison and his attitude to the people among whom he sojourned for his sport.

34
Folklore New Every Day

Nearly forty years after the "Iolaire" disaster I was set thinking about it again by a comment made by a Norwegian professor at an international conference on Celtic folklore.

He said we should not regard folklore as something belonging to the past. Something concerned with heroes and fairies, giants and witches. Folklore, he said, is being created every day. It is a potent influence on our lives.

He instanced some of the folklore which came out of the wartime resistance movement in his own country. Perhaps the prime example of the potency of folklore, and myth, is the state of Northern Ireland today.

Neither the IRA nor the Orangemen are living in the real world, and every new incident their subservience to myth involves them in, produces its own new folk tales, and its own new atrocities.

The most widespread piece of folklore arising from the "Iolaire" was the widely held belief that the Captain and crew were drunk.

Having regard to the inexplicable nature of the disaster, and the time of year, the suspicion that drink was involved was natural.

It was probably given an added impetus by the political background. Prohibition was a live and emotive issue at the time. Stornoway was on the run in to its six dry years.

The public inquiry which was held after the disaster disposed of the story pretty effectively. The jury's finding was not a simple negative, that they found no evidence of drink. It was the quite positive statement that no one on board was under the influence of intoxicating liquor.

The jury included one at least of the leaders of the Prohibition movement in town who would not have subscribed to such a finding if he had any reason to suspect that the demon drink had a hand in the disaster.

But still the story persisted. Perhaps still persists.

Other much more unlikely stories also linger on.

I have heard it asserted, on more than one occasion, that there were high words between the Captain and some of his Lewis passengers at Kyle before the vessel sailed, and that the Captain was heard to threaten, "I'll dip their heels before they get to port."

Even after the Admiralty archives were opened up to inspection and the facts were finally known, an elderly crofter gave me a circumstantial account of an incident at Kyle on the day of the disaster which he claimed to have witnessed himself.

It wasn't as simple as the version I have given above, but in a very indirect, allusive, periphrastic manner, he tried to create the impression that the Captain was determined from the start to sink his ship.

The crofter was not a Lewisman — the folklore of the "Iolaire" is not so localised.

He was one of the Raasay raiders. A descendant of those who were driven from the relative lushness of Susinish and Fearns to the harsh sterility of South Rona, where many of their sheep died of hunger among the rocks.

After the first World War, he and his companions took forcible possession of their old lands on Raasay, and, after a period in gaol, were re-settled there by the old Board of Agriculture.

In spite of these far fetched tales the significant fact about the "Iolaire" is the relative absence of folk-tale and myth. The wound was too deep to be wrapped around in that way.

My father began his account of the disaster in the "Gazette" with the words, "No one now alive in Lewis can ever forget the 1st of January 1919."

He was not thinking simply of the recollection of an event, but of a searing experience which warps or purifies the mind.

It is something the inhabitants of a mining village can understand, or another seafaring community. Shetland for instance. But not the floating population of a large city whose sorrows are discrete and personal, rather than corporate, however intense they may be.

Although I was not touched directly by the "Iolaire", I still live under the shadow of that New Year morning, as does everyone else of my generation in Lewis.

It is not just that I was at an impressionable age when the tragedy occurred, nor that I am unduly sensitive or given to brooding on the past.

It is rather that my own response to the disaster has been intensified by the silent grief of those who felt it even more than I, echoing and re-echoing round me. Not in spoken words, but in attitudes, gestures, dress, and sombre habits of thought.

We are creatures of memory, looking at life through cumulative layers of our own experience, and, in an island community, through the experience of those around us, (even those who went before us,) and who are part of us, just as we are part of them.

The oldest of my aunts, not long before her hundredth birthday, spoke to me about the change that had come over the attitude of the older women of Lewis to colour in her own lifetime.

When she was young, she said, the women were fond of gay colours. Even the elderly. It was only gradually the habit grew up of wearing black excessively. A habit we have now largely grown out of again.

I may be wrong but I have a feeling that, over the same period, the mood of the island in religious matters became less buoyant, more grim and gritty.

The explanation of the change can be found, in part at least, in the "Iolaire" disaster.

The argument can be pushed too far. There were black clothes in Lewis before the disaster, and there have been light hearts since. Our religious attitudes have older and deeper roots. But no one could live in Lewis over the period I am writing of, without realising that there is a folk memory, and that we cannot understand why people think and act as they do, unless we know what the content of that memory is.

In Lewis, for those of my own generation, and older, the folk memory is charged with disasters and set-backs, some of which I have referred to. Others I will deal with later.

101

The people of Lewis until comparatively recently, have fought a bitter rearguard action against a harsh and ungenerous environment, and hostile outside forces.

These influences have been compounded by the disproportionate effect of two world wars, and the "Iolaire" disaster.

Those growing up in Lewis now find the island a much more kindly and hopeful place. They have never been forced by circumstances to choose between predestination and despair. They are no longer haunted by the drum beat from the past.

But perhaps, in some ways, they are all the poorer for that. There is certainly no evidence that they are happier, or more deeply attached to their native island.

Affluence and freedom may prove to be harder taskmasters than the disciplines we knew in the past.

35
The Eagle's Horn of Plenty

Unfortunately I am not familiar with the Gaelic poetry which has grown up around the "Iolaire", but I am not aware that anything has been written which carries with it the cumulative horror of the catastrophe, apart from the poems of Murdo Macfarlane, Melbost, who witnessed the immediate aftermath as a boy.

Within a few days of the disaster Jack Maciver, who wrote intermittently for the "Gazette" over a long period of years, composed an elegy in English which has the great merit of being completely unpretentious.

The first verse, and the last, will serve to sum up what he had to say:

"'Home at last!' they whispered, as glowed the shore lights bright;
   'There lies the bay, and Arnish Light is gleaming through the night;
Go, get your kit bags ready, for the voyage now is o'er,
   And grand will be our welcome on our well-beloved shore.
Home at last!'

"So near their home, and yet so far that never, nevermore
   They'll roam the dreaming moorland or by the lone sea shore —
Theirs be the calm of heaven, the peace the world denied,
   After Life's cruel tempest — the hush of eventide.
Home at last!"

A few months later Neil Munro wrote his "Prologue Spoken by the Players". It was recited by Sir John Martin Harvey, the celebrated Shakespearean actor, at a gathering in the King's Theatre, Glasgow, organised by the Highland Societies in the city to raise funds for the dependents of those lost in the disaster.

I was unfamiliar with the poem until I came on it by chance leafing through the old files of the "Gazette". I found it very moving.

The first and fourth verses give the gist of the poem.

"April has come to the Isles again blithe as a lover,
   Shaking out bird-song and sunshine and soothing the tides;
April has come to the Hebrides, filled them with frolic,
   Only in Lewis of sorrow, bleak winter abides."

"They had lit up their windows for beacons, the women of Lewis,
   The peat fires were glowing a welcome, the table was spread;
The sea brought their sons back from war and the long years of tumult,
   And cast them ashore, on the cliffs of their boyhood, dead!"

But it is the second verse I think of most frequently:

"Always they went to the battles, the people of Lewis,
And always they fell, in the wars of a thousand years;
Peace never to Lewis brought Springtime of joy or of season,
The wars might be won, but her women were destined to tears."

Not having learned anything of the history of my native island at school the significance of the verse eluded me when I read it first. Since coming to the mainland I understand it better.

I cannot go to Elgin without driving through Auldearn, where the National Trust for Scotland commemorate a battle in which more than three hundred Lewismen lost their lives. In fact only three escaped. The mainland chief who led them into it changed sides almost as soon as the battle was over, but that was too late for Lewis.

I cannot motor to Kyle by Invermoriston without passing another National Trust signpost, marking the site of the battle of Glenshiel where, according to Sir Walter Scott, several hundred Lewismen were engaged in the abortive Jacobite rising of 1719. An odd, confused and bungled affair during which, oddly enough, Eilean Donan Castle was defended by Spanish soldiers beseiged by the British navy.

Both Jack Maciver's poem and Neil Munro's have a folk quality in that they are simple direct expressions of what the community knew and felt, but they are both in English, and are almost unknown in Lewis where the only poem which has gained a measure of oral currency hovers uncertainly between MacGonagal and the ballads.

In 1960, when I compiled a short account of the "Iolaire" disaster to meet a public demand arising from the unveiling in 1959 of a memorial at Holm Point, I collected several variant versions of it.

In some of the versions Arnish Light had become Ranish Light. In one version it had become "the Cornish Light".

The poem had evidently passed through the hands of people who did not know the story independently and were unfamiliar with the locale.

The last three verses will suffice.

"They fought for Britain's glory
They've sailed the ocean o'er
But at last they died like heroes
On the threshold of their door

"And, all their warfare ended
They've laid their armour down
They have won the British laurels
And today a heavenly crown.

"Their storms in life are over
Their anchors safely cast
In that celestial harbour
With God himself at last".

The presumption is that the poem was written by a Gaelic speaker. The problem is why it was written in English, and how it gained currency among people whose deeper thoughts were more naturally expressed in Gaelic.

It is a mystery related, no doubt, to the fact that, although the name of the ill-fated vessel is the Gaelic word for eagle, it was not generally recognised as such by the Gaelic speakers of the island.

Sent out from their schools illiterate in their native tongue, they read it as English, and gave it the completely meaningless pronunciation I-o-lair.

The final irony and absurdity is that "Iolaire" was not the vessel's real name. She was the "Amaltheia", called, presumably, after the foster mother of Zeus, to whom was presented the original horn of plenty, with the promise, in abundance, of whatever the heart might desire.

The "Amaltheia" was sent to Stornoway to replace the Stornoway depot ship, the real "Iolaire", a yacht which belonged to Sir Donald Currie. To avoid confusion, the Admiralty gave the new depot ship the name of the old.

There is reason to believe that some of those who were lost in the disaster had elected to sail in the "Iolaire", thinking it was Sir Donald Currie's speedy and comfortable yacht.

Although the names of those lost in the disaster were included in the bronze panels in the Lewis War memorial, it was only forty years after the disaster the island got round to erecting a memorial at the spot. It was done largely on the initiative of Allan Cameron, North Tolsta, and without very much general support.

It was around the same time the first real poem about the "Iolaire" was written, by Iain Crichton Smith.

Smith was not born when the "Iolaire" was lost. He got his facts from an account of the disaster which appeared in a Canadian magazine in 1956, from which I published quotations in the "Gazette". He was responding to the trans-Atlantic echo of a disaster which had occurred a few miles from his Lewis home.

His poem, which appeared in the "Saltire Review" is a relatively straight forward account of the disaster, but the questions it raised stayed with him.

A few years later he came back to the theme in his poem, "After the War", published in his collection "Thistles and Roses".

> "After the war had said its last
>   and they were sailing into frantic arms —
> to have been stunned by their own Lewis seas!
>   One cannot speak of this
> or ask the illuminating storms
>   to write their reasons on a plain coast."

Paradoxically, because of changing attitudes and beliefs, it may be more difficult to come to terms with the "Iolaire" disaster now, than it was when the wound was raw.

36
The Crofter's Premiere

The Folklore Conference which set me thinking about the "Iolaire" disaster from a new direction was itself a memorable occasion. It was attended by forty delegates from universities from Iceland east to Finland and as far south as Italy.

Since the establishment of the Comhairle gave the islands some independence, and our membership of the EEC gave our affairs an international dimension, we have become fairly well accustomed to conferences of that sort in the islands. But in the fifties it was breaking new ground.

The conference was organised by an old Nicolsonian, who had been a classmate of mine for several years, Neil A. R. Mackay. He was then the British Council representative in Scotland.

Secretary of the local advisory committee was Alex Urquhart who had been our class teacher when he first came to the Nicolson nearly thirty years before. It was very pleasant for the three of us to be working together again, in a slightly different relationship from that in which our friendship was first formed.

Associated with the conference there was an exhibition in the Town Hall at which one of the exhibits was some of the Uig chessmen on loan from the Scottish National Museum.

In recent years the Uig chessmen have become one of the most widely known works of art in Britain, thanks to the replicas sold by the British Museum, and the replicas of the replicas, produced by countless craftsmen up and down the country.

But, until that exhibition, sponsored jointly by the British Council and Glasgow University, the chessmen had not been seen in Lewis, even in replica, for well over a century.

I knew of them only by hearsay. I had never even seen them in the British Museum. I had no idea what they looked like.

But I did know that they had been exhibited for many years in the British Museum as chessmen from "Uig, Isle of Skye". A mistake to which the attention of the Museum staff was directed by an Uig student at London University, Malcolm MacLean, an uncle of Stephen MacLean, who, like Stephen himself, died prematurely, without realising the promise of a brilliant university career.

There was one incredible session at the Folklore Conference. An argument blew up between the Welsh and the Irish as to which was the older and purer representative of the aboriginal Celtic tongue. It seemed to hinge on one or two obscure consonantal sounds. It was all very technical and abstruse, but so much enthusiasm was engendered it sounded like a wild political brawl, conducted in a language from outer space.

The most memorable session for me was the afternoon on which Duncan Macdonald, a crofter, from Peninerine, in South Uist, recited for the assembled delegates a Gaelic folk tale which had been handed down orally in his family for more than three hundred years.

Duncan was introduced to the gathering by Calum Maclean from Raasay. What a contribution he and his brothers have made to Gaelic and, indeed, to European culture, as poets, folklorists and scholars!

"There is many a poor man in Scotland
   whose spirit and name you raised:
you lifted the humble whom the age put aside",

wrote Sorley Maclean in the English version of his Elegy for Calum, whose early death was a great loss to the islands.

Certainly it was true that afternoon. The recital was held in what was normally the Reading Room of Stornoway Public Library. Calum Maclean set the stage for Duncan Macdonald's story. He gave the audience Duncan's genealogy, generation by generation, back to the early seventeenth century, when his family were hereditary bards to the Macdonalds of Sleat.

He showed how, when the bards lost their power, as a result of the Statues of Iona in 1609, Gaelic culture went underground. The Highland crofters kept alive the songs, stories and poems of their people — a rich heritage. Most literate Scots thought of them as ignorant and uncultured. That was a reflection of their own ignorance. They did not have access to the crofters' minds.

At the time of the conference, according to Calum Maclean, there were perhaps half a dozen seanachaidhs still left in Gaelic Scotland of whom Duncan Macdonald was probably the best. He had in his repertoire more than a hundred traditional and heroic tales, many of them requiring an evening or more for their recital.

To listen to this gentle, humorous, courteous and dignified crofter, was one of the most moving experiences of my life, although I could not understand a word of what he said, having been educated into ignorance of the culture he sustained.

He told his story with an occasional simple gesture of the hand, but obviously with great, though restrained dramatic effect. When he concluded, the gathering of savants from all over Europe applauded as if they had been attending the premiere of some great new work of art in one of the leading theatres of the Western world.

A Scandinavian professor spoke of Macdonald as one of the last representatives of the oldest literary tradition surviving in Europe.

One of the Irishmen said sadly that it was like being present at the death bed of a culture.

Duncan, I was told, showed his courtesy and his humour a few days later when he gave another recital at a gathering in Oban in connection with the National Mod, then in progress.

He was tackled at the end of his story by a critic in the audience, who said he had heard him tell the tale before, but on this occasion he had forgotten part of it. His memory couldn't be all that good.

Duncan smiled and replied, "I did not forget. But on this occasion there are ladies present."

I did not discover what, in the Oban story, Duncan considered unsuitable for feminine ears.

Something of the old culture has been saved from time and the vandals by men like Campbell of Islay, Alexander Carmichael, John Lorne Campbell of Canna, and latterly by the younger men of the School of Scottish Studies of whom Calum Maclean was one.

But to understand the islander it is necessary to remember that his history is almost as fragmented as his geography. He has been violently detached, more than once, from his cultural roots. The bloody-mindedness which obtrudes occasionally in his religion, as in his drinking, is in part a consequence of that alienation.

Excessive drinking has many causes, and they may operate differently in different situations. Excessive social drinking, for instance, has a different history from the reliance on alcohol to provide "Dutch courage" when, for some reason, one feels inadequate.

My own experience suggests that a proportion of Gaelic speakers, (especially in my youth when Gaelic was still exclusively the language of the home in rural areas,) resorted to drink before transacting simple matters of business, because they felt themselves at a disadvantage in dealing with unfamiliar matters, in an unfamiliar tongue, with people who might be inclined to sneer at them, or put it over them.

The choice, of course, is not between a closed Gaelic culture and an open English educational system, and it has never been.

Agnes Mure Mackenzie remarks in one of her histories that Greek was taught in Lewis before it was taught in the High School of Edinburgh. Kenneth Clark in his book "Civilisation" makes the point that Western culture survived through a critical period only in the inaccessible fringes of Cornwall, Ireland and the Hebrides.

The in-growing, self-regarding, pathetically boastful attitude which sometimes disfigures the Gaelic movement is a product of decay. The desperate thrashing around of a drowning man.

It gives no indication of the manner in which the Highlands might have developed if Gaelic and English had been allowed to find their own balance in an unforced way.

More importantly, it gives no indication of how the situation may evolve if those who are seeking to use Gaelic for cultural (as distinct from political and personal ends) are given the financial support and encouragement they need.

Or what contribution the Western fringe with its strong sense of community may yet make to a civilisation in which technology is getting out of hand, and individual freedom is degenerating into anarchy.

37
An Admiralty Whitewash?

Perhaps this would be an appropriate point at which to pick up some of the facts and comments which have come to me in letters from near and far, correcting, corroborating or amplifying what I have said.

When I wrote some weeks ago about Murdo Gow, the ladies tailor, who was one of those who gave the Stornoway of my boyhood the flavour of a real town with real idiosyncratic people in it, I had no idea that he had been trained in Paris.

The information has come to me in a letter from a niece of his in Greenock whom I never had the pleasure of meeting, which is not perhaps surprising, because she grew up in Shanghai where she was, in her own words, "imbued with the tales and traditions of the Lews."

Mrs Armour writes, "My grandfather, also named Murdo Macdonald, was Factor to Sir James and Lady Matheson at Lews Castle. Lady Matheson was so impressed with young Murdo Gow's flair for tailoring that she sent him to Paris to be trained as a couturier.

"My father, Duncan Macdonald (Dunkie Gow) was a seventh son who was supposed to have healing power. Eight years later my aunt, Flora, made her debut. All the brothers emigrated except Murdo. Flora married a Dr Foster and spent her married life in England."

Mrs Armour's father was for forty years in the employment of Butterfield and Swire. Latterly he was Commodore Chief Engineer of the Line. Among his close contemporaries in Stornoway were Kenneth Mackenzie, who founded the tweed firm of that name, and George Mackenzie who emigrated to Grand Rapids Michigan, and became a prominent businessman there.

"Unfortunately I never met my uncle Murdo," writes Mrs Armour.

I was not able to give her much more information about him than I had used in my article, but I was able to tell her that I had met her father on one of his visits to Scotland from the Far East.

I was a student in Glasgow at the time, and we met at the "Lewis and Harris" of which Dunkie Gow was a life member, despite his sojourn in the Far East.

The Annual Gathering of the Lewis and Harris was an even more prestigious affair then than it is today, although it is still one of the premier events in the island calendar.

An uncle of mine had come up from England for the occasion, and I can still recall the smile of pleasure which crossed his face when he, quite unexpectedly, bumped into Dunkie Gow, one of the companions of his youth.

My regret is that I did not listen more attentively to their night of reminiscence about old SY.

I was switched to a different scene by a letter from California.

Donald MacLeod, brother of "Easthy" and "Neilan", one time pipe major of the

109

Stornoway Pipe Band, writes, "I would have been one of the small fry in your company when you went to Brevig to meet the fishing boats."

He was commenting on my reference to having been given a skate by one of the skippers, when I was on holiday at Back schoolhouse with Ian Morrison, the headmaster's son.

"One of the busiest and most successful boats was ours, and it was with my father that Ian played hooky, and went out fishing, when his mother thought he was somewhere else. How I envied him, going out fishing on these long summer evenings when I had to go fetch the cows from the moor."

Ian, he says, was their leader in their efforts to procure sports equipment, not easily come by in those days.

"On Hallowe'en evening the bunch of us got together, acquired two burlap sacks, and then went from house to house. We walked in the door — no knocking in those days! — recited our "rann", and the householder, or usually the lady of the house, gave according to their means. A penny! Two pence! Sometimes as much as sixpence!

"If money was short, and it usually was, they gave us a basin of potatoes. When enough potatoes were accumulated, some kind carter took them to town for us and sold them to a grocer — no charge for the service! When we had enough money we sent to Bennet Finks for whatever ball we could afford.

"In the Ian Morrison years he insisted that we keep on until we had enough for a football with square panels. The first in the Back school. Were we proud?"

Donald comments that he has no idea whether the same custom was followed in other parts of the island. The villages had so little contact with each other. "Once a year to the Drobh was as far from home as we got."

"Changed days at Back," he adds, "and all the other island schools. Junior teams, intermediate teams, senior teams. With equipment supplied! I bet we had more fun."

He comments, truthfully, that I grew up in Stornoway in "the Maori and country Lourag years" when many people in town considered it degrading even to know a "low grade language like Gaelic," and when, as he adds, some country folk pretended to an ignorance they did not have, for the same irrational reason.

He leaves a question with me which I cannot answer.

"What is a lourag?"

I have no idea of the derivation but I can feel the scorn with which it was used.

A more serious issue is raised in a letter from Stornoway. Jacky Morrison expresses his disappointment that, after the secrecy restriction on the papers relating to the Iolaire disaster was removed, no one saw fit to question the findings of the Admiralty Inquiry.

"It is obvious," he comments, "that the Admiralty Inquiry was a whitewash to deflect blame from their Lordships and their officers."

"It is astonishing that the captain and officers of a ship that was wrecked with such appalling loss of life should have been found blameless. Yet that was, in fact, the conclusion of the Admiralty Inquiry.

"Indeed, the only people their Lordships found reason to criticise were a couple of civilian taxi drivers.

"Also the remark by one of their lawyers that 'there were enough fishermen available to man the lifeboat twice over' was a quite deliberate attempt to apportion

110

blame to men who were sleeping in their bunks wholly ignorant of the disaster.

"The loss of the Iolaire, and the deaths of over two hundred men was the fault of the captain who left the bridge when the vessel was nearing Stornoway, leaving an officer in charge who was unfamiliar with the approaches to the harbour.

"There is no evidence that after the ship struck any action by the Captain or his officers saved life. Ashore there were no facilities provided by the navy for saving life from a stranded vessel, and no action by the Commander or his staff at the Naval base at Stornoway saved life.

"No mention was made in the Admiralty Inquiry of the body of the Captain of the Iolaire being found on Sandwick Beach wearing two lifebelts. There are reliable witnesses still living who can testify to this shameful fact."

Jacky Morrison, as one of the leading skippers in the Stornoway fishing fleet, is well qualified to comment.

I have some reservations about the two lifebelts, not having heard the story myself from eyewitnesses, but it may be true.

That apart, I endorse his strictures on the Admiralty Inquiry as a cover up.

There was in fact another Inquiry. A Public Inquiry before a Sheriff and jury. Its findings were almost identical with Jacky Morrison's comments.

The jury unanimously concluded "that the officer in charge did not exercise sufficient prudence in approaching the harbour, that the boat did not slow down, and that a look-out was not on duty at the time of the accident; that the number of lifebelts, boats or rafts was insufficient for the number of people carried, and that no orders were given by the officers with a view to saving life."

The jury also found that there was a loss of valuable time between the signals of distress and the arrival of life-saving apparatus in the vicinity of the wreck.

The Admiralty case did not go by default at that enquiry. Both the Admiralty and the Crown were represented by advocates from Edinburgh as well as local solicitors. The hearing lasted two days, and they had every opportunity of cross examining the witnesses.

The Admiralty Inquiry, in fact, was exposed as a whitewash before it even took place.

The disaster had causes as well as consequences, and they should be on the record, but my primary concern in writing has been with the latter.

It happened almost in a moment more than sixty years ago, but we can still feel the reverberations.

38
The Admirals Confused Me

Memory plays strange tricks.

In an earlier article I suggested that the cup presented to Stornoway Golf Club by Admiral Tupper was no longer competed for because someone had won it outright.

A letter from a Stornoway golfer, now assures me that the Tupper cup is "alive and well" and played for annually. It was the Boyle cup which was won outright, by Angus Macleod, formerly of the College of Agriculture.

Why on earth did I confuse Tupper with Boyle? Could two names be more unlike?

The answer is simple. Boyle was also a golfing admiral, so the two cups were always bracketed together in my mind. Whether Boyle preceded Tupper in charge of the Stornoway naval base, or succeeded him, I cannot recall, but they were both part of the background to my childhood.

It is by associations of this sort, drifting from one topic to another that these reminiscences are being written. That is the way memory works. Our knowledge of a place is always partial and associative. We know the same place differently at different times depending on which set of bells have been set ringing in the memory. This approach also highlights the inner-relatedness of events — something we tend to lose sight of in a busy urban environment with a rapid turn-over of friends and associates.

For instance, the information about the Golf Club's trophies come to me in a letter from Norman Macgregor, whose father was librarian in Stornoway and one of my closest friends for many years. A letter from Norman sets off a whole train of memories, right back to the night his father was appointed librarian in the early twenties.

I was just a youngster at the time. I had never heard of Dan Macgregor, and had never seen his native village of Tolsta Chaolais. But I can still recall the ring of pleasure in my father's voice when he came home from the Library Committee meeting and told us an appointment had been made, and he thought it was a good one.

I got to know Dan soon after that, when, as a schoolboy I discovered P. G. Wodehouse. I might say I discovered them both at the same time. Over the years I got as much fun from the one as from the other. But the fun with Dan was real. He will figure once or twice in the story, as I proceed.

It must have been around the time of the Folklore Conference I have been writing of, although quite unconnected with it, that he told me how he had seen the door of the library toilet open, and five black clothed cailleachs emerge, one after the other, having shared a penny. Like Wordsworth's daffodils, "they stretched in never ending line." Dan just couldn't believe it was physically possible for the place to hold them.

Pennies were pennies then, and there was no other convenience in town a woman could use.

The Conference itself illustrates the inter-relatedness of events. It had consequences projected into the future which no one could possibly have foreseen.

At the end of the conference, the Town Council entertained the delegates to a dinner in the Town Hall. It was quite a splendid occasion.

I was asked to propose one of the toasts. I think it was to Glasgow University, one of the joint sponsors. In any event it seemed a good opportunity to do a little canvassing on behalf of the islands.

Glasgow University had just begun to do extra-mural work within the city. It was a new departure at that time. I made a plea for the remoter areas, suggesting that the need increased with the square of the distance. Lack of know-how has always seemed to me an even greater barrier to development than lack of money.

The point was taken, and, shortly afterwards, Neil Mackay and I were invited to Glasgow University to meet the Principal, Sir Hector Hetherington, to discuss the matter further.

I cannot recall anything about the meeting except the pride with which I told the company over dinner that, if they listened to the radio of the following night, they would learn that my old school had won the BBC "Top of the Form" contest in competition with schools from Scotland, England, Wales and Northern Ireland.

The captain of the Nicolson team was Ronald Urquhart, whose father had been associated with us in making the local arrangements for the conference. The other members of the team were Alasdair Maclean, Ian Mackay and William MacTaggart.

As a result of our discussion that night, Glasgow University decided to take Lewis under its wing, and, for a year or two, programmes of extra mural lectures were arranged. Eventually, however, it was decided that the islands belonged to Aberdeen, geographically, rather than Glasgow.

The short-lived Glasgow connection, did have one lasting result.

The final event in the first series of meetings was an "Any Questions?" session in the Town Hall, with the questions being answered by a team of academics.

One of the questions posed was "Who were the Picts?"

Three of the academics had spoken, and I wondered if there was anything left to be said on the subject when the fourth speaker rose. His reply delighted me.

"I object to the question", he said. "Who *were* the Picts? I *am* a Pict."

He proceeded to give us one of the best discourses on the Picts I have ever listened to.

His name was Alastair Fraser, and, in a very real sense, I believe that was the first link in a chain of circumstances which eventually induced him to give up a good post in the University and become a teacher at the Nicolson Institute.

One might almost say that he came to Lewis on the bow wave, or in the wake (which is a consequence of the bow wave) of the folklore conference. With one of his sons now taking a pioneering interest in fish farming on the scale most appropriate to a crofting community the consequences are far from worked out yet.

I have one other vivid memory of Glasgow University's extra-mural involvement in Lewis, although it does not have the same sort of antecedents and consequences.

A learned professor of medicine gave a most interesting series of talks on his own speciality, but at one school on the west side he came up against a phenomenon he

113

had not encountered before — an islander taking the Mickey out of an unsuspecting visitor.

At the end of his talk, he invited questions.

One of the audience rose. He might have been a crofter. In fact he was the headmaster of a nearby school. He began a solemn interrogation of the professor from an extreme fundamentalist point of view.

"If the good Lord sends an epidemic of smallpox to wipe out the population of Lewis, what right have you to interfere?" he asked.

The professor, — Allsop, I think was his name — treated the question seriously and courteously, explaining the situation simply, as if he was talking to a child.

"If the Lord has given me the power to cure disease," he concluded, "my use of that power is surely part of the Divine purpose. Think of all the lives that have been saved because doctors can cope with epidemics."

"That's all very well," persisted the pseudo fundamentalist. "We know how many people die of smallpox. But how many die of doctors?"

It was at that point the worthy professor began to realise that a Lewisman is not necessarily as simple as he seems.

39
Manco and Cutch

Shortly after I received Norman MacGregor's letter, which brought back to mind the two golfing admirals — Tupper and Boyle — I spent a holiday with my brother in Warwickshire.

His memory of Stornoway in the First World War is much sharper than mine for two very good reasons.

He is three years older than me to begin with, and three years makes a mighty difference at that stage of life. When War broke out he was nearly twice as old as I was!

But also, he left Stornoway when he went to University at the age of 17, and has not been back except for short holidays. His recollection of Stornoway between 1910 and 1925 is not blurred and cluttered as mine is by the recollection of everything that has happened since. He recalls it as it was.

When I mentioned the Admirals, he reminded me of the Manco — the naval depot ship which lay in Glumaig during the First World War. One of its functions was to provide a wireless link with ships at sea in the Minch or the Atlantic.

Wireless at that time had a limited range, and communication between the Admiralty in London and ships at sea was complicated.

There was no radio link or even trunk telephone between Lewis and the mainland. Messages passed to and fro in Morse tapped out on little brass buzzers in the Post Office. There was a cable across the Minch to carry this telegraph traffic. It came ashore at Branahuie where the lonely little "cable house" was a prominent landmark. Periodically the cable was cut by a careless trawler scraping the bottom of the Minch, and Stornoway was isolated from the mainland for days or even weeks on end.

Communication between the Manco and the shore base in the old Imperial Hotel was maintained by the Sea Cadet Corps, or, as it was at that time, the Navy League.

Rain, hail or shine the lads of the Navy League stood on the point of Number Two wharf with their signal flags hatched in red and yellow, relaying messages by semaphore for onward transmission by wireless.

At night they used Aldis lamps.

The Navy League was the only youth organisation in Lewis at the time, and it attracted many of the brightest boys in town despite its very close affiliation with St Peters to which few of them belonged. It was for many years the largest, or second largest, unit of the Navy League in Britain.

Many of those who stood on the Point of Number Two, in the First World War with their signal flags, had good careers in later life. One of them was Donald Maclean who became Commodore Captain of the Cunard Line when it was still, probably, the most prestigious shipping company in the world.

The harbour was always busy in those days with naval launches hurrying here

115

and there. I can't help feeling, in retrospect, that "aye they seemed busier than they were."

On one occasion I was in a small boat with some of my contemporaries. We could not have been more than six or seven at the time. We were lying in the naval berth, where we should not have been, when a launch came bearing down on us.

We panicked, and began to row in different directions with the result that we went round in circles where we were, right in the path of the oncoming launch.

An older boy, Dan the Slip, saw us from the pier, scrambled down one of the iron ladders, and jumped on board to take charge.

If I remember aright he pushed us under the pier, out of harm's way, until the launch had berthed.

From the Navy League, and the Manco my brother and I went on to talk about our games.

With the free run of the streets we all had hoops until we outgrew them. Wooden hoops from herring barrels which bounced and ricocheted on the untarred streets. Or old bicycle wheels sans tyres, and often sans many of their spokes.

At one stage we had proper iron hoops made for us by Keith Macdonald the blacksmith. His house was just across the street from ours, but his smiddy was down in Bell's Road.

I had forgotten, until Eric reminded me, that Keith had a huge iron cone outside his smiddy for making hoops and metal tyres for country carts. The hoop or tyre was roughly shaped on the anvil, then heated red, and beaten down on the cone until it was a perfect circle.

Was I proud of my iron hoop!

I didn't even have to propel it by hitting it with a stick as I had propelled other hoops in the past. With the hoop I was given a little iron gadget, hooked at the end. Once I had learned the trick it was possible to hold the hoop with the hook and birl it along without the necessity of striking it. In our eyes, as boys, it was a sort of Rolls Royce among hoops.

We called the gadget a "streeler" not realising that we were corrupting, and perhaps misapplying, a Gaelic word. I always associated the name with the screeching sound of iron on iron as we ran with the hoop.

It is only since I began this excursion into my memory that I have come to realise that my boyhood English was permeated with Gaelic to a much greater extent than I would have believed possible. This is something I must come back to later.

The next building to Keith's on Bell's Road was another smiddy. I can't recall who had it then, but I knew it well, at a later stage, as Ossian Macaskill's. Next again, going down towards Newton was a barking shed. No monofilament nets in those days!

The fishermen had to soak their herring nets periodically in hot cutch to preserve them. It was this process that gave the nets their characteristic brown colour. Even more than the colour I remember the smell — a warm astringent wash house smell.

Even when I knew it first, the barking shed was beginning to go out of use. As steam drifters took over from sailing boats the crews did their barking on board, generally at weekends when they had hot water running to waste.

As one walked along the piers the smell of the cutch frequently caught the attention before one had spotted the crew at work.

Next to the barking shed there was a cooperage. The presiding genius at that time was Jimmy Campbell, always popular with the boys.

He was a source of interest, too, because on one hand he had two thumbs.

Many years after the period I am writing of, he was a patient in Lews Hospital under the expert care of Norman Jamieson, the surgeon, to whom so many Lewis people owe so much. But he too had a debt to pay, as it turned out.

One day, as he stood by Jimmy Campbell's bedside, he asked the patient, "Were you ever in Lerwick?"

"Yes," came the reply.

"Were you there in such and such a year?"

"I was."

"Did you by any chance pull a youngster out of the harbour when he was in danger of drowning?"

"I did."

"Well," said the surgeon, "I was the boy."

He recognised the hand that had saved his life.

40
Skills of a Vanished Race

One of the advantages of growing up in a small town like Stornoway in the early years of the century was the free education one got, wandering round the piers and the workshops, seeing how things were made, or done.

Coopering was a highly skilled trade. Especially in the days before the barrel staves were bought machined and ready from some highly mechanised British or foreign yard.

In the old days the cooper had to cut each stave himself. It had to be bent exactly to the barrel's shape, and tapered along the sides to fit in place beside its fellows. The whole thing had to be done so precisely that the barrel was watertight when it was put together.

The staves were held by five hoops. There were metal hoops at the top and bottom. The bottom hoop held the circular base firmly in a notch cut in each stave an inch or so from the base. The top hoop was only put firmly on when the barrel was closed. It locked the lid in the same way, in a groove.

The three hoops in the middle were made from long strips of some pliable wood which could be bent around the barrel. Again the skill of the cooper was shown in the deftness with which he notched the withies he was using, so that, when he wrapped them round the barrel, the ends interlocked and held the hoop secure without a nail.

We would watch the coopers for hours as boys, aspiring to their skill. Aspiring in vain, as far as I was concerned. I was never good with tools.

The sawmill on Lewis Street, to which I have already referred, took us a long step on the road to mechanisation. It was powered by producer gas, made on the premises by passing steam over red hot coke. The chuff chuff of the engine was audible over a wide area. It told us when the place was busy and there was something for a boy to see. The waste gas had a characteristic smell which is with me at this moment but which I cannot describe.

Perhaps the most memorable feature of the sawmill was the agonised screech of the logs as the revolving blade ripped through them.

One of the things which interested us was the machine which printed the names of the kippering firms on the little slats of wood from which they made their kipper boxes. Printed in red, or blue, the bits of wood poured out, proclaiming the virtue of Louis Bain's kippers, or Duncan Maciver's or Woodger's, as the case might be.

The sawmill was a cosmopolitan institution. Sharpening saws at the carborundum wheel — how we loved the flying sparks — was Bauer, a Swiss. The manager, Walter Lees, was a Yorkshire man who came to Lewis by mistake.

He saw a post advertised in Lewis, thought it was in Lewes in Sussex, and applied. When the job was offered to him he thought he might as well see a remote part of the world at someone else's expense, and took it, planning a short stint, a sort of working holiday. He stayed for the rest of his life.

In fact he married a local, one of the Gerries, a farming family, and became the only Englishman to be a Bailie of the Burgh of Stornoway. An achievment which cannot be repeated because the burgh and its bailies have disappeared into the dustbin of history.

By coincidence another Yorkshire man is taking an active part in the new regime as a member of Comhairle nan Eilean, and showing the dogged character of his race by standing firm on the unpopular side of the Nato debate.

Shortly after he came to Lewis, Walter Lees went exploring the rural areas on his bicycle. Down in Bayble or Garrabost he ran over a hen. When he had picked himself up after the spill he reported the accident to the owner, an irate lady who demanded five shillings for her loss. Five shillings was quite a bit of money in those days but Walter Lees paid up to avoid an argument. The woman took the money and moved away, picking up the hen as she went.

"Just a minute," shouted the canny Yorkshireman. "That's my hen! I've just bought it for five shillings."

He retrieved his prize, and took it home for his landlady to cook.

From the sawmill, when we were in search of something to occupy our minds, we might cross the street to Norman Forbes's joinery, or go round into Church Street to the wheelwrights, on Keith Street Corner, just across from Murdo Macrae, the butcher's, shop.

It was fascinating to watch a wheel being made for one of the country carts. The climax of the operation came when the blacksmith was called in to put the metal tyre around the rim.

The blacksmith was on the other side of the street — in fact there were blacksmiths all over the town, in Bells Road, Church Street, Scotland Street, Keith Street and Bayhead.

The blacksmith lit a circular fire to heat his metal tyre. When it was ready it was slipped over the wooden rim, and quickly dowsed with water, to tighten it, and prevent the wood from catching fire.

The smell of burning wood, the cloud of steam and smoke, made almost a ritual of the occasion. At the same time we were learning in the most practical way possible, that metals expand with heat. When Roddie Macrae set up an experiment for us in the school lab to prove the point, it was all old hat. We had already learned our science on the street.

I don't remember who the wheelwright was in those days, or who the blacksmith on the opposite side of the street. But I knew a later incumbent of the smiddy well. Like most of the tradesmen in the town in my youth, and later, Steallag was a great man to have a yarn with. Full of fun.

I remember him stopping me one day to tell me of a horse which had gone missing. Was it from the Manor Farm? Or was it from Laxdale? I can't remember. Anyway it vanished.

While the owner was making fruitless enquiries for the errant animal in the vicinity of its home base, the horse was on Church Street in Steallag's smiddy getting shod. It had cast a shoe, and without waiting to be taken, set off on its own to the blacksmith's a mile away, where it knew the discomfort could be remedied.

I was always fascinated by Stellag's door. One of his main jobs in his latter years was making horn brands for the island's sheep. When each brand was ready, he heated it red hot, and burnt it into the door just to make sure that the letters and figures were right.

I hope that door has been preserved. It is a piece of social history.

On occasions Dugald Maclean, who for many years occupied the butcher's shop which had been Murdo Macrae's in my youth, used to send sheep's heads to Steallag for singeing. His message boy, one day, finding the smiddy temporarily deserted, left a sheep's head on a sheet of metal on the floor, and wrote, with the blacksmith's chalk, the explantation, "This is Dougie's head."

Dougie enjoyed the joke even more than Steallag. In fact it was he who told me of the incident when we were next door neighbours on Matheson Road.

Having learned about the expansion of metals by watching the blacksmith and wheelwright, we learned about inertia by watching Johnny Og, or Warhorse, taking the rolls or loaves from the oven, steaming hot, with a long flat wooden paddle.

What child today knows any delight to compare with a fistful of hot bread, straight from the baker's oven, gouged from the end of the loaf your mother had sent you to buy?

Or even the lesser delight of seeing your new pair of trousers being made by the tailor, sitting cross legged on the floor, in a corner of his room, raised like a platform on which to perform his minor miracles?

Or of discussing politics, theology, or the latest practical joke, with a roomful of shoemakers, sitting on their wooden stools or benches, in their long leather aprons, with a last on each knee — and each mouth full of nails?

41
They Hid the Diamonds in a Barrel

I have a good memory for location, but a bad memory for chronology. I cannot remember the sequence of events in time. Sometimes I cannot even be sure whether something of which I have a perfectly clear recollection happened five, ten, or fifteen years ago.

But I do associate events with places. Books I have read away from my own fireside remain with me better than books I have read in my usual surroundings. My recollection of the book is reinforced by my recollection of the place and circumstances in which it was read.

When Joe Flett wrote a novel, and I reviewed it for the "Gazette", I read it in the train between Inverness and Perth. I could not guess even wildly at the date, and I have no recollection of the purpose of my journey. But I recall incidents from the story, although I have completely forgotten many more memorable books I read before and since.

The trick by which Joe Flett's stolen diamonds were smuggled out, concealed in a barrel of salt herring, is inextricably associated in my mind with the rough texture of the cloth with which the third class compartments (as they were then called) were upholstered; the smell of smoke and the soft black snow of smuts in the old steam trains, and the moving landscape between Inverness and Perth.

The ruse with the diamonds was a natural for Joe Flett. He belonged to one of the leading familes in the herring trade. Flett was a name to conjure with when I was young. But he seemed to have no interest in the family trade — except for literary purposes.

When I used to meet him, and exchange a passing greeting, on his solitary walks through the Castle Grounds, I had no idea he was gestating a thriller, until the publishers sent me a copy, and the story became confused in my mind with a journey through the Central Highlands.

In the same way events are associated in my memory with the rooms in which I experienced them, or heard of them first. If I had moved house more often, I might have remembered more!

There was a small patch of woodworm, or dry rot, in the floor of one of the attics in the old house in Lewis Street which is associated in my memory exclusively with one event — the great gale of 1921.

The room had been the maid's room for the short period when we had a maid who slept in. Later I was permitted occasionally to sleep in the attic myself. I always had a sense of adventure, sleeping up there on my own, in a room with a sloping roof, away from the rest of the family, with no one even on the same floor. It must have been a nuisance for my mother to climb an extra flight of stairs each day to make the bed, or take up a tray to me when I was ill, but she indulged me occasionally.

121

My sense of adventure was heightened when one day the castor of the bed at the corner nearest the door, poked through the floor and set the bed atilt. Thereafter we had to be careful how the bed was placed, to keep it on the plumb.

That bedroom was a good setting for an eerie experience, such as I had in it.

My usual bedroom on the floor below has warmer associations in my memory. Sitting up in bed to watch for the rockets greeting Lord Leverhulme, as I have already said, or groping excitedly in the dark for my stocking on Xmas morning.

The blind search for the bar of chocolate I expected to find at the top of the stocking, and the bulge at the toe which was surely an apple, or that greatest of luxuries, an orange, relate to a room with blue Regency-striped wall paper, and a map of Canada on the wall, which was the basis of our guessing games when we had a long lie on Saturday morning. A guessing game which made me much more familiar as a child with the place names of the North West Territory of Canada than those of my native island.

The Xmas bedroom had no sloping roof, no hole in the floor, and, oddly, in my memory, no gales.

Lewis is one of the stormiest regions in the world. There are few winters when gusts exceeding a hundred miles an hour are not recorded. At the Butt of Lewis, since statistics have been kept, the wind has reached gale force for an average of twelve hours a day during the months of December and January.

I must have been conscious of gales while I slept in that bedroom as a child. Admittedly it was sheltered. It was not on the corner of the building, and had only one fairly small window, but it did face west, the direction from which our severest gales approach.

I think the reason why there were no gales in the Xmas bedroom is simply that in a region of continuous high winds in winter we forget, or ignore, the ordinary gales. We remember only those that stand out like Himalayan peaks. The gales against which later gales are measured, and of which tales are handed down from generation to generation.

I know of the gale in which the Newton house was unroofed by family tradition. Although even my mother could not remember it herself, I can almost hear the voices shouting to the stricken vessel, "Gilsland ahoy!" and the waves beating on the beach in a white fury. In some ways it is more vivid to me than those I experienced myself. It has a heroic, legendary quality, just because I was not there, and my imagination can ascribe to the scene all the feelings of exultation and fear I have known when battling with other gales, without being fettered by a precise knowledge of observed facts.

In a modest way I suppose I am stepping up Bella's gale in my mind much as a Balzac or a Tolstoy heightens everyday existence by creating imaginary people, and imaginary events, more real than life itself.

The great gale of January 1953 was just as severe as either of the earlier gales, but then I was a grown man, recording the event as a journalist, as accurately as I could. It lacks the almost supernatural quality of the family tradition, or the gale I listened to from my attic bedroom as a child. But by any standard it was a memorable storm.

Exercising the magic power which the typewriter confers, I will postpone the onset of these great gales to a later issue.

In the meantime I must raise a question which I cannot answer but which others may.

122

To what extent has the wind become a more significant influence on life in Lewis since the old thatched house, so perfectly streamlined, has been replaced with square boxes and picture windows designed for softer climes and adopted by us in an effort to keep up with the Jones's, irrespective of the weather?

How far on the other hand has the loss of streamlined houses been offset by the shelter of the motor car?

The Swedish lady my mother once met in Bournemouth had the right idea. When she heard where my mother came from, she looked at the sunny promenade, shook her head, and remarked, "The wind will be very big up there."

Big it is, and big it will be. But sometimes it is bigger than others as in 1921 and 1953.

42
What Happened to the Red Crusader?

It was the last Friday in January 1953. I had gone to a meeting of the Stornoway Trust. The night was blustery but not unusually so, and, after the meeting, we planned to go to a Lewis Hospital Ball.

I never had any confidence in my own skill as a dancer. A fact I have always regretted. Dancing was then, and I suppose still is, an important social accomplishment. I used to suffer agonies of indecision, whether to sit out still another dance, or make an exhibition of myself in the middle of the floor. It was, I suppose, a form of inverted egotism. I don't suppose anyone really noticed what I was doing on the dance floor, except, perhaps, the poor girl whose toes I was standing on. On this occasion I had little choice. As a member of the Hospital Management Committee I felt I had an obligation to be there, and my dinner jacket was laid out on the bed before I went to the meeting, ready for a quick change whenever it was over.

The meeting had not properly begun when the maroons were fired calling the lifeboat. I slipped out quietly and went round to the Lifeboat Station where the crew were already gathering. By this time the wind had freshened preceptibly, but it still gave no hint of the fury to come.

I was told that a light had been seen by coastguards off the north of Skye. It appeared to be a distress signal and the lifeboat was called to search the area.

I sent a brief message to the daily newspapers and went back to the Trust meeting. It would be some hours, I knew, before the lifeboat could have anything to report.

The Hospital Ball, of course, was out, so far as I was concerned. I had to stay beside a telephone. It was one of the many occasions on which Cathie had to accept (and placidly did so) that a journalist, if he is married at all, is inevitably a bigamist. He can never divorce himself from the news.

The best thing, I decided, was to snatch a little sleep, setting the alarm to waken me about the time the lifeboat might be expected back. Long before that, I was wakened by a thunderous hammering at the front door.

I hurried down in my pyjamas and found a friendly policeman come to tell me that my telephone had been blown down, and the Glasgow Herald was trying to get in touch with me about a vessel which had sent out distress signals from the west coast of Lewis, somewhere near the Butt.

This was another story altogether, and but for the policeman, I might have slept right through it. The police office must have been one of the few still in contact with the mainland at the time. Telephone lines were down all over the island.

When I went to get the car out there were occasional flurries of snow and a wind such as I have never experienced before or since. It was a struggle to open the garage door. It was a greater struggle to keep the car on the road across the Barvas moor.

When eventually I stopped, I was blown ten yards backward before I got the handbrake on.

When I got to Borve I could see the lights of a large vessel close inshore. The "Clan MacQuarrie". She was in ballast, rearing high out of the water. A perfect target for the vicious wind. She had been driven helplessly on to a reef.

The Lifesaving Crew from Stornoway were on the scene by this time. They had to leave their vehicles and manhandle their gear, including an electric generator, for about a mile across a broken moor to get near the wreck. They were pushed here and there by the wind. Flung into ditches. Battered with hail and flying spray. When they tried to signal to the wreck with an Aldis lamp, it took three men to hold the signaller steady. The wind was now gusting well beyond a hundred miles an hour, and a huge wave drowned the generator, plunging the rescue team into total darkness. There was little they could do but wait for daylight.

I returned to Stornoway. There was no telephone on the west side in working order from which I could send a message.

By this time the lifeboat had returned to base after a fruitless search off Skye. The crew was standing by in case they had to make a second journey in the same night, round the Butt to Borve. A frightful prospect in the prevailing conditions, but they seemed to take it in their stride.

Later I learned that a Fleetwood trawler, the "Red Crusader", had vanished that night with all hands. She was known to be somewhere in the Minch, but was not supposed to have been in the area where the coastguard saw distress signals. No one will ever know what happened to her.

I also learned that there had been what seemed at first another major calamity. The East Coast fishing fleet, tied up for the weekend at Ullapool had been blown from its moorings. Scattered like a miniature armada and piled up on the beaches. Something like seventeen vessels were involved. At least that is the figure that sticks in my mind. Surprisingly the wind and the rocks were kind to them, and the damage turned out to be much less than had been feared.

The good news about the fishing fleet was some hours in the future. In the meantime there was the "Clan MacQuarrie", on a lee shore, with more than sixty men on board, in imminent peril. I will never forget the sight that met my eyes when I got back to Borve.

Crofters and fishermen had gathered from all the villages along the coast. Big burly men who had lived with the sea all their lives. The Lifesaving crew had got a line aboard the "Clan MacQuarrie", and a hundred willing helpers were holding it taut, as the bosun's chair shuttled back and fore above the breakers.

Every man on board was taken safely off. Even the ship's cat. And they didn't get their feet wet.

It was the biggest rescue by breeches buoy in the history of the sea, up to that time, at least, and so far as I know, it has not been surpassed since then. The Lifesaving crew were later awarded the Board of Trade shield for the best rescue service of the year. A modest acknowledgment of a magnificent job, in which all the villages along the coast played a part.

It was one of the most exciting stories I ever handled, but it didn't make the front page in the next morning's dailies. The value of news is relative. There are no absolute standards. The interest of the public in an event depends on the other events it is competing with at the time. The rescue at Borve seemed pretty small beer to news editors at city desks who were receiving around the same time, reports that the Stranraer Ferry, "Princess Victoria", had been caught in the same gale, and sunk with appalling loss of life.

The comparative news value of the "Clan MacQuarrie" and the "Princess Victoria" is easy to understand. The disaster overshadowed the rescue. But later, in another context, I will have occasion to tell how another exciting sea story was killed, so far as the dailies were concerned, because a prominent Cabinet Minister was caught the same day leaking budget secrets.

There was a belated bonus in the "Clan MacQuarrie" story, however, so far as I was concerned. The mate, who was left in Borve to keep an eye on the wreck, married the postmaster's daughter.

After disaster, romance stands highest in a newsman's scale of values.

43
When the Lintels Flew

The gale which wrecked the "Clan MacQuarrie" was fierce but honest. The gale of 1921 was freakish and deceitful. It had more the quality of a cyclone, or tornado, then a straightforward Lewis wind, blowing free across the unencumbered ocean.

I have heard graphic tales of it over the years up and down the Highlands. Everyone spoke of it as unique in their experience. The Captain of one of the fishery cruisers told me many years later how he had been caught that day in East Loch Tarbert. The haystacks were blowing over the ship like smoke.

I was in bed with a cold when the gale struck in the little attic room. I knew something strange was happening outside. The noise of the storm was tremendous. I was afraid the window might come in at any moment. Then my mother called me out of bed to go to the window and look. The roof of the picture house was coming up the street, towards us, chest high.

The wind had lifted half the corrugated iron roof off the Picture House beside the Seminary, in one solid piece. It was carried round from Keith Street into Scotland Street, and then into Lewis Street. It finally came to rest against the railing of Maggie Macneil's house on the corner of Lewis Street and Scotland Street.

Next day, when I was up and about again, I was astonished to see that a garden shed in Scotland Street had been lifted bodily over a six foot wall and was now standing, still apparently intact, in the grounds of the Free Presbyterian Church.

There was a similar incident in one of the villages round Broad Bay — Tong, I think it was. A fishing boat, with the lines and bait aboard, ready to go to sea, was lifted by the wind and carried up the beach for a hundred yards. It was dropped there, still on an even keel, without a line or hook displaced.

A lintel from the burnt out Town Hall was flung across the street through the window of what was then the Waverley Hotel. It smashed the dining room table. It was surprising that the wind could move so large a stone for such a distance. More surprising still, the dining room table was on the first floor of the Hotel — above the level from which the lintel had come.

It was not quite so surprising that the tall chimney stacks of the pagoda-like Fish Mart came tumbling down one after the other. Or even that a house in Aignish was destroyed. Several lives were lost. The children old enough to be at school survived. One of them was later a classmate of mine, for a number of years, in the Nicolson. She emigrated to Canada with quite a number of my classmates in circumstances which will form part of my story in due course.

In Marvig the gale destroyed the local shop. There was no loss of life, but the contents of the shop, including the heavy iron weights used for measuring out potatoes and flour, were carried a considerable distance by the wind. In Leurbost one very surprised old lady, going to the byre to see that the cow was safe, was lifted out of her unlaced boots, and carried through the air for several yards.

Mrs Drummond, a stout little lady, whose husband was in charge of what was then known as the Combination Poor House was caught by the gale when she was shopping. She was blown over, and birled along Bayhead Street like a top.

When my brother came home at lunch time he told us that in the middle of their examination — he was sitting his "Intermediate" that day — the room was suddenly filled with oak chips from a kipper house in Newton which had been wrecked. They had to blow chips off the page as they wrote.

When my father came in he described for us what he said was the most terrifying and exhilarating sight he had ever witnessed — the stragglers of the fishing fleet, caught by the storm in the Minch appearing and disappearing in the welter of water at the harbour mouth, as they raced for shelter. Fortunately they could make harbour.

Stornoway is always accessible, and the Inner Harbour must provide some of the safest berthing in the world for small craft. This is what has made the town of Stornoway. There are few fishing ports in Britain so well endowed. Nearly a square mile of enclosed water, with an open entrance, free from rocks or bars or other obstructions; a deep water anchorage under the lee of Arnish Point, and an inner harbour curled round on itself like a winkle shell so that it is completely sheltered from every wind.

Nature enabled Stornoway to live with the gales of the North Atlantic as few of the other fishing villages on the west coast of Scotland could, dependent as they were on open beaches, or narrow fiords with treacherous squalls funnelling down between the hills.

The town was first created by the facts of geography, but the men who have lived there, from the Vikings to the present day, have made it what it is. The native-born nucleus provides the continuity from one generation to the next. Assimilated incomers from the rural hinterland or across the Minch provide much of the character as well as the power to adapt.

Among the incomers have been seafaring families with exotic names like Ryrie, Pope and Crockett which have become part of the history of the town.

The Ryries I have already mentioned in connection with the Ness fishing disaster. So far as I know there is no one of the name now resident in Lewis, but a Moderator of the Free Church, the late Rev. Angus Finlayson once told me that he was a great grandson of Capt. Phineas Ryrie's daughter.

So far as I know there are no Popes in Stornoway, as I write this. The last of the family was Mary Pope well known to many school generations of Nicolsonians.

In my childhood, however, part of the North Beach Quay was still referred to by East Coast fishermen as "Pope's Corner", because Dan Pope, from Devon, via Rothesay, had a sail loft there a century ago.

There are still Crocketts in Stornoway, some of them localised by marriage as Macdonalds and in recent years they have given the town two lifeboat coxswains who have been decorated for rescues which required consummate seamanship and courage of no ordinary kind.

By coincidence, while I was writing this the "Gazette" came to hand with an account of the presentation of the silver medal for gallantry of the RNLI to Coxswain Malcolm Macdonald for the rescue of 29 seamen from the "Junella" in a force nine gale.

I reported myself the two occasions on which another Callum Macdonald — his uncle — received the same award.

On the first occasion he took the lifeboat into a narrow gulley at Sulisgeir to pick up a stranded party of guga-hunters. The Captain of a Fishery cruiser which was standing by at the time told me he shut his eyes, afraid to look. He did not believe that any vessel could venture in among the rocks in the prevailing conditions, and survive.

On the second occasion Callum Macdonald and his fellow crew members rescued a young couple from Lochs, whose boat was wrecked on the Sgeir Mhor. They were in danger of being drowned at any moment by a rising tide breaking fiercely over the reef, as, indeed, their older companion was, when he attempted to get a line across to the lifeboat.

This rescue was watched from the shore by hundreds of helpless bystanders, who knew the Sgeir Mhor, and its grisly history, and had no illusions what the odds were against success, or even survival, as eight men staked their lives for two.

On that occasion in fact there were three "Crocketts" in the crew — Callum Macdonald, the Coxswain, who received the silver medal, John Macdonald (Callum's brother and Malcolm's father), the assistant mechanic who received a bronze medal and Malcolm Crockett their cousin.

44
A Fire and a Mystery

The confused chronology of this exploration of my memory has led me to blow away the lintels of the burnt-out Town hall before I have set fire to it, or even built it.

The fire and the building are both part of the story, the latter more significant than the former. The building, however, was before my time and I will start with what I know and saw.

The Town Hall was in use, in the first World War, as Admiralty Offices and a Naval Canteen. There was a strongly held belief in town that the building was fired, deliberately, to destroy incriminating documents. What these were supposed to be I never heard specified. Perhaps someone was thought to be fiddling the Canteen accounts.

So far as I know there is absolutely nothing to support the local rumour. It has never taken much, in the way of fact, to germinate a rumour in Stornoway. A simple act of carelessness, such as might well occur among the staff or the clients of a busy canteen, could have started the blaze. Once the building was alight it was clearly doomed. The walls were panelled with pitch pine and riddled with gas pipes.

Even in a town accustomed to tarred kippering sheds catching fire with monotonous regularity — especially when times were bad! — the Town Hall fire was a memorable blaze.

I watched it from an attic window in Stephen MacLean's — just opposite St Columba's church. We looked down across the roof tops of Keith Street and Francis Street, on a glowing brazier which had been Stornoway's pride and joy — the clock tower. The flames leapt high above the town, and the sparks seemed to light up the whole sky. Suddenly the clock tower vanished into the bowels of the ruined building. The flames and sparks rose higher than ever, as if celebrating their triumph of destruction. As I watched, from a seat in the "gods", so to speak, my father, with the ambivalent attitude to every story of the local journalist who really identifies with his community, was simultaneously 'covering' the fire, and helping his friend Hugh Miller to retrieve the Parish Council records from the blaze.

They got out of the building seconds before the clock tower fell.

By coincidence, just after I had drafted this, I had confirmation of my recollection of the spectacular nature of the fire from an unexpected source. A long interesting letter recalling several of the incidents and people I have already mentioned, or will mention later on. The letter was from Kennedy Cameron whom I last saw more years ago than I would care to confess to. He is a good deal younger than I and watched the blaze as a child from his home in the Bank House just along the street from the Town Hall.

"I can still see the flames shooting across South Beach towards the harbour," he writes. "We were too close for comfort and were evacuated to — of all places! — the

Gas Works. I think Mrs Millar was a distant relative of my mother. I remember being rather scared of this move as my young brain had dreamed up the possible horror of the gas pipes in the Town Hall bursting into flames which would surely travel through the pipes right to our refuge in the Gas Works.''

Whether any incriminating Admiralty accounts perished in the blaze or not, a good many of the historical records of Stornoway and Lewis were lost, and the whole of the public library.

For most of the years of my youth the Town Hall was an empty shell. The walls of reddish, warm Isle Martin stone were blackened by smoke, but still standing, a little uncertainly. Inside the building there was nothing but heaps of rubble, and the rusty doors of the strong rooms, drunkenly ajar.

When the Town Hall was destroyed the various public bodies which had used it had to seek new accommodation.

The Library was housed for a time in the hall of Martin's Memorial Church. A few shelves of books in a corner of the room represented what had once been a very fine municipal collection.

Later the Library moved to the old Seminary on the corner of Keith Street and Scotland Street. It was approached down the passage between the Seminary and the Picture House. One then went down some steps into what had once been a class room. It was there I first got to know Dan Macgregor.

The Town Council found refuge in the Masonic Hall. The Council, I have been told, became the custodians of some crates of liquor, confiscated during Stornoway's dry spell. When the time came for the Council to move into the new Town Hall, the tally of bottles was correct. But, strangely, they were empty.

I can only say of the incident what has been said to myself on innumerable occasions, when I have pressed an informant to authenticate his story — "If it's a lie to you, it was a lie to me." It was a Town Councillor who told me. A Town Councillor, moreover, who might have had a shrewd idea where the liquor went.

Whether that tale is true or not, it is true that, when the flitting took place, Archie Munro, the venerable Town Clerk, attempted to carry with him to the new Town Hall the gas mantles the Council had been using in their temporary home.

You could buy a gas mantle for a few pennies. Anyone old enough to remember gas mantles will know how fragile they were. After a mantle had been lit for the first time, and the protective coating was burned off with an acrid smell, the merest puff would destroy it. How the Town Clerk ever expected to carry them safely from the far end of Kenneth Street to South Beach is a puzzle. Why he wanted to do it at all, is an even greater puzzle, for the new building was lit by electricity.

But they were public property and he would not contemplate leaving them behind.

The explanation of Archie Munro's aberration is, I think, old age — which creeps up on all of us. An able and upright man, who served the community for many years with a granite probity which is rare today, he was beginning to become a parody of himself.

Not long after the move into the new Town Hall I was the witness of a painful scene as a cub reporter. Archie Munro had suffered a bout of temporary amnesia. He had no recollection of a short emergency meeting the Council had held. At the next meeting, when the minutes were asked for, he stoutly denied that the meeting had ever taken place. With complete lucidity, and considerable eloquence, he defied

131

the united efforts of nine town councillors, and his own assistant, to presuade him to record in the Council's Minute Book the decision that had been taken. He was not going to falsify the Minute Book with a fictitious entry!

I have frequently regretted over the years the loss of public documents in the Town Hall fire. There seems to be hoodoo on the island's written history. Many of the ecclesiastical records, which would be invaluable today, went to the bottom of the Minch in circumstances I will have occasion to mention in another context.

Apart from the written records we also lost in the Town Hall fire the two sticks of red pine which had been used as a calendar by Malcolm Macdonald and Murdo Mackay from Ness when they went, as modern hermits, to Rona, in May 1884, following a Church dispute at Ness.

Two boats went from Ness that summer with friends, trying to persuade them to return, but they refused. Nothing could be done during the long winter, and in April 1885 when next it was possible to effect a landing, they were both dead. Macdonald was in a sitting position beside an improvised fireplace in the crude stone bothy where they had spent the winter. Mackay was lying on the floor beside the fireplace, with a tartan plaid spread neatly over him.

The sticks were given to the Town Council by Dr J. L. Robertson, a Stornoway man who became Senior Chief Inspector of Schools, and who has already been mentioned obliquely in my tale. They were notched on each corner for the days of the week, with a deeper notch for Sunday, and a cut across the face of the stick for each month. The last few notches were less clearly cut than the earlier ones, and they ceased altogether on Tuesday, 17 February, 1885, a little over a month before a party from Ness effected a landing on their third attempt to approach the island after the winter storms.

45
The Provost who might have been a Peer

The story of Stornoway's first Town Hall, formally opened in September 1905, is interesting in itself, but it could easily lead us to the Parliament Act of 1911, to some "lost" cantos of Dante's Purgatorio; to a meeting of the Convention of Royal Burghs in the reign of Charles I; or to a lonely creek on the Gold Coast where the master of a ship lay dying, attended by my grandfather, his brother-in-law and mate.

It will not be possible to follow these threads simultaneously, but they will all be woven into the fabric in due course because they are inter-related.

The Town Hall represented monumentally, in stone, the changing relationship between Stornoway and rural Lewis, and the general ebb and flow of the island's fortunes during the period with which I am most concerned. It was a sort of three dimensional metaphor of the island's general history.

It was built on a great upsurge of civic pride at a time when Stornoway was governed by exceptionally able men, all of them natives, some of them known not only locally but nationally.

It stood a stark and dismal burn-out ruin through the dreariest and most depressing decade in the island's recent history, the symbol of a dying town for which there seemed to be no future.

It was rebuilt, in a somewhat more subdued mood than the original hall, when Lewis began to pick itself off the floor at the count of nine, and confound the critics who had written it off.

And it finally became redundant, at least for its original purpose, when the town and island — or, in this context one should say, town and islands — ceased to be separate, and sometimes antagonistic, administrative units with the formation of the Comhairle.

The Comhairle itself, at least so far as Lewis is concerned, was a belated recognition of the revolution wrought by the motor car and the bus, which fundamentally altered the relationship between town and country, marrying the two with a rare intimacy where previously they had merely been juxtaposed.

The civic pride which brought the first Town Hall into existence was embodied in the legendary provost of my very early youth — John Norrie Anderson — one of the ablest public men Lewis has ever produced. Almost certainly the ablest Lewis was able to hold within the local stage. I can see him before me as I write — full blooded, vigorous, passionate (in both senses of the term) with a jaw thrust out like the prow of a ship.

And yet I wonder whether I am really remembering him, or piecing the man together from the familiar portrait which hung in the Town Council Chamber, and the stories I have heard about him from my father and my older playmates.

My father had an almost unqualified admiration for him although he was well aware of Anderson's failings, and they were failings which were particularly repugnant to him.

My father based his life, and his work as a journalist, on the principle that a man's personal frailties are a matter between himself and his maker.

The function of a local newspaper was to report public events fully, and truthfully, and to maximise the value of an able man to the local community by backing up whatever good he sought to do.

Stories about Johnnie Anderson were legion. I remember some of the older boys describing a scene they had witnessed at the harbour. Rightly or wrongly, I locate it at No. 3 wharf, Stornoway's vanished greenheart pier, which thrust out towards Goat Island from a point near Shell Street. There was a slant on the west side of the pier from which small boats could be launched at any state of the tide. Johnnie Anderson, as I visualise him in the story, stood at the top of the slant, shouting imperiously for "Four oars and a boat!" I don't know what incident in the harbour had occasioned his dramatic call for a boat, associated in my childhood mind with Shakespeare's, "A horse! A horse! My kingdom for a horse!" The point of the story, as the boys told it, was that he became so excited eventually he was calling for "Four oak boats and an oar." Which we thought was hilariously funny.

As I put it down now, with a cynical adult mind I wonder whether in my innocence, I missed the point. Perhaps my older contemporaries, who had seen the incident were relishing the fact that the worthy Provost was a little under the weather. His great career as a civic leader certainly did end under the shadow of drink. Norrie Maciver once told me how he was sent, as a youth, by his father on some errand to Anderson's office. When he reported that the ex-Provost, as he was then, was immured alone with a bottle, his father refused to believe him, and gave him a row for spreading scandalous stories.

In his earlier years Johnnie Anderson had been a dominant and respected figure in the Convention of Burghs.

During the constitutional crisis over Lloyd George's radical budget which laid the foundations of the welfare state, his name was listed by the national press among the prominent public figures who were to be made peers, if it became necessary to flood the House of Lords with Liberals to get the legislation through.

My father spoke with respect, almost with awe, of Anderson's ability to comprehend an intricate document in a single glance. While others were still struggling to spell it out, bogged down in detail, he would have isolated the only points that mattered, and be ready with his reply. On one occasion, when the mailboat, presumably the "Sheila", was very late, Anderson regaled the crowd huddled in the Fish Mart with a stirring recital of "Marmion" from begining to end, from memory, although he had not read it since he was a boy at school

In many of the stories he was seen as the champion of the community against overbearing strangers. We used to thrill as youngsters at the story, still current in the town, of his confrontation with the Sheriff, nearly twenty years before, when King Edward VII visited Stornoway. The Sheriff stepped forward to greet the King as he came ashore from the pinnace. Anderson restrained him, and moving forward in his place said, "After the Provost of Stornoway, if you please!"

I do not know who the Sheriff was, nor what protocol demanded in the circumstances of the visit, but Anderson was Stornoway, and the Sheriff was the hostile world outside, and we admired our champion.

There was another story of a quarrel he had with a local figure who had a builder's business. Anderson's rival tried to annoy him by breaking his office windows one night from a discreet distance, with a sling. Next morning Anderson was at the builder's yard looking very crestfallen, complaining of what "these damned boys" had done to his windows, and pleading for a speedy repair. As soon as the job was done, he was back in the builder's yard with the curt message, "Don't send me a bill! And don't do it again!". He never had any doubt who the culprit was.

Although he figures in this way as one of the heroes of my youth, passing from history into folklore as we spoke about him, what I have still in quite sharp focus are the letters he used to write my father after he went to live in Edinburgh.

I always associate his removal to Edinburgh with his weakness for the bottle. He lived out the few years remaining to him in the city, cut off from all he had worked for in his native island, apart from an almost clandestine correspondence he kept up with my father, writing often on scraps of brown wrapping paper, or torn up grocer's bags.

There was an element of tragedy in the situation, but a letter from Johnnie Anderson was still a great event. My father would take it home and read it to us over lunch or tea. We would listen with bated breath to some shrewd comment on a public issue of the day, or a long excursion into the byways of local history. I remember particularly his contribution to a long debate about the birthplace of Sir Alexander Mackenzie, the explorer; his account of the last duel in Scotland, fought at Goathill Farm; and his fascinating account of the Mutiny on board the "Jane".

His copious store of history and tradition spilled over the fragments of paper on which he was compelled by circumstance to write so that, when the page was finished, he wrote round the margin, and often on the back of the envelope, so that one reached the end of the story before the beginning.

46
The "Nuclear Issue" of 1908

Johnnie Anderson's letters from Edinburgh, written on scraps of paper, were far in the future when his great ambition was achieved, and Stornoway's first Town Hall was opened in 1905.

The site had formerly been occupied very largely by stables, but the new building was a fine one by any standard, especially for a struggling little fishing town like Stornoway. And it was opened by an ex-Prime Minister, who was accompanied by a member of the Cabinet, and a galaxy of peers.

In assessing the significance of that we have to make a time adjustment. Today a Prime Minister can fly from Heathrow to Stornoway in much the same time that it takes him to go by car from Heathrow to the House of Commons. In 1905 Lord Rosebery and his party had to make a journey of several days by sea and land to honour a town which was then, truthfully, remote.

Stornoway was en fete for the occasion. The buildings and the ships in the harbour were decked with bunting. The town was illuminated at night, and there was a display of fireworks. Even the warring factions in the Council buried the hatchet for the day. When the town's Artillery Brass Band, under Sgt. Major Craig, led the gathering in the 100th Psalm, Johnnie Anderson was supported on the platform by his arch enemy, Aeneas Mackenzie, and by William John Mackenzie the builder who was alleged to have broken his office window with a sling.

The harmony was short lived. The building was still encumbered with debt. The Council owed the British Linen Bank £4500. It seems a trifling sum by today's standards, but three quarters of a century ago it rocked the town. The interest on the debt amounted to something like sixpence in the £ on the rates.

When a group of local businessmen suggested that the problem could be resolved by letting the hall as a licensed restaurant there was an uproar. There was a very active temperance lobby in the town. The debate raised moral and emotive issues as deeply divisive as current debates on nuclear weapons or the culling of seals. The Council argued for months. The town was in a ferment. Then the arena was changed. It was decided to consult the ratepayers, and the battle was staged in the Town Hall itself.

The meeting was held more than two years before I was born, but I could almost persuade myself I was there. The echoes were still resounding through Stornoway in my youth. I have heard the meeting described by my father. I have read his detailed report of the battle more than once. Most of the protagonists were known to me.

The proposal to let the hall was sponsored by Kenneth Mackenzie founder of the tweed firm which still bears his name. He had found a client for the hall prepared to offer a rent of £500 per annum. Stornoway, pursuing a temperance policy along the wrong track, had over the preceeding few years cut the number of licensed premises in town from 16 to four. This did not reduce the drinking but it did increase the profits. The Town Hall as a licensed restaurant would be a very attractive proposition indeed.

On practical, financial grounds, Mackenzie made an excellent case. His was an impressive and closely argued presentation, although he did ruffle some feathers by one or two unnecessary personal jibes. He was supported by John Macritchie Morrison and Angus Bain, the joint founders of the sawmill on Lewis Street. On the other side of the argument there was an even more formidable array of talent led by Anderson himself, although the eloquent climax of his speech, in which he spoke of the misery and degradation drink could cause, reads now like an ironic foreshadowing of his own decline.

He was supported by Peter Macleod, baker, one of a family known locally, and not without reason as the "Smarts". My father used to tell of an occasion on which Peter and his brother took opposite sides on the land question, then a burning issue. One of them invited a leading Irish Land Leaguer to Stornoway to support his case. The other was present in the audience and subjected the speaker to a devastating cross-examination. Next morning my father met the Land League brother and asked him (as tactfully as he could) how he thought his meeting had gone. The reply was direct and uninhibited, "I was sorry for my speaker, but, by God, I was proud of my brother."

Another prominent opponent of the proposed restaurant was Bailie Murdo Maclean, founder of the drapery and furniture firm, although at that time his interest was mainly in the fish trade. He dealt extensively in salt ling from Loch Roag.

Far and away the best speech of a lively evening was made by Dr Donald Murray, who later became the first M.P. for the Western Isles, and quickly established a reputation in the House of Commons as an orator. His was a hard-hitting, well argued speech, seasoned with humour.

"My friend Mr Mackenzie is a gentleman I respect. He calls a spade a spade. Why does he call this pub a restaurant?"

There was a stormy scene towards the end of the meeting when Alex Morison, a well known Land Leaguer, mounted the platform to voice some personal grievance against Johnnie Anderson. At first there was confusion, but then he proceeded to address a series of questions to the Provost.

"Have all the remittances received been lodged in the bank in a separate account?" he demanded.

"Yes!" said the Provost. "I hope Mr Morison has accounted for everything he has received."

"When is this begging and sponging operation to end?"

"When the debt is paid."

"When are the ratepayers to get a list of the subscribers?"

"Tomorrow morning on application to the Town Clerk."

"When is it to be published in the press?"

"The sums received have already been acknowledged in the press and your name does not appear among the subscribers."

When the uproar caused by this exchange had subsided the meeting got round to a vote.

John Macritchie Morrison suggested that there should be a referendum. He was supported — for very different reasons — by Roderick Smith, the chemist, who was not on the council then but later gave many years of service to the burgh, and was one of the pillars of the temperance movement.

The proposal for a referendum was carried.

The supporters of the restaurant thought they had scored a victory, the ratepayers were sure to support them.

They cheered lustily when the figures were announced.

They had made one small but vital miscalculation. They forgot Stornoway's sense of humour.

47
The end of the Town Hall Pub

It was not the suggestion that the Town Hall should be let as a licensed restaurant that aroused Stornoway's mirth, but the suggestion that when the debt had been paid, the Council should take it over, and run it themselves for the common good.

"Your muddy streets will be paved," the ratepayers were told. "Your dim gaslight will give way to the brilliance of electricity. A modern refuse destructor will be erected. Stornoway, in short, will become a model town without costing the ratepayers a penny more than their present rates."

The echoes of Kenneth Mackenzie's eloquence had hardly died away before the whole town was reciting with relish a newly minted poem.

"Come list ye Stornoway Ratepayers, a song to you I'll sing
  Of how you can abolish rates and every nasty thing,
And get your streets all paved with gold, and banish all the mud,
  By voting straight for Kenny and the Town Hall Pub.

"No longer will the 'Ocrach' your balmy air pollute,
  A grand refuse destructor will render Dannie mute;
And if you catch the fever — a bairn or wife or hub —
  Will be nursed in a braw new hospital from the Town Hall Pub.

"What matters though the fishing fail and trade be very slack,
  You do not need to worry 'bout burdens on your back,
The workman need not labour, and the housewife need not scrub,
  We're all to be made millionaires by the Town Hall Pub.

"No longer need the lamplighter his almanac peruse,
  To see what time the moon is veiled, and then apply the fuse
To gas lamps out of date. If you cause this scheme to bud
  You'll have grand electric arc lamps from the Town Hall Pub.

"Why should we leave to strangers the task of making drunk?
  It is a home industry the town is wrong to funk —
Our sons can learn to drink and our topers drain their tub,
  In a college of our own in the Town Hall Pub.

"What matters if the drunkard's child should cry aloud for bread!
  What matters if — as oft occurred — the father's brought home — dead?
To widows' groans and orphans' cries we'll turn our deafest lug,
  He saved us three halfpence a pound in the Town Hall Pub!"

The poem — if poem it is — settled the matter. It was all too good to be true. Stornoway laughed and voted the proposal down.

The town was still laughing over the incident ten years later or more. I could recite snatches of the "Town Hall Pub" as a boy, and some of my older school friends could recite it all.

The story of its origin, as I have heard it, is that it was written by a local handyman gardener, whose name I do not recall, if in fact I ever heard it. He showed it to Dr Murray, whose garden he tended, at what was then known as "the Cottage," on Church Street almost opposite the Drill Hall. Later the building was enlarged and converted into a school hostel. Murray arranged to have the poem printed and distributed. Then he went round to my father's office to tell him that the fuse was lit, and await the explosion.

"But how," asked my father, "did you distribute the poem without the risk of Kenny seeing your hand in it?"

"Very simply", said Murray. "I posted parcels anonymously to the three men in town who dislike him most."

The ruse worked. Murray's part in it was not suspected. But that did not protect the poor printer. I have heard my father chuckle many times over the trembling figure which arrived at the office sometime later, seeking advice and solace, as many of the townsfolk did, in time of trouble.

The "Ocrach" referred to was the public refuse dump right in the centre of the town, where the Bowling Green is today. Unsightly and offensive to the nostrils. "Dannie" was Donald Maciver who had a shop on Bayhead Street almost immediately opposite the "Ocrach". He campaigned continually to have it closed down, but he was long dead before the city fathers grassed the area over, and moved the "Ocrach" to the other end of the town, to reclaim Young's pond at the back of Seaforth Road, as they had reclaimed the estuary of the Bayhead River.

The reference to the lamplighter perusing his almanac has an interest of its own. It was the habit, right into the thirties, to light the street lamps only when there was no moon. No moon according to the almanac that is. There were many nights when the moon was shining somewhere above a thick band of cloud while the citizens groped around in the dark because the city fathers were saving on the gas. It was only when the town went over to automatic clocks, in the early thirties, that the old custom was abandoned, and even then there was a vigorous rearguard action by the economy brigade.

I remember Ian Maclean, with whom I used to go for long walks late at night in those days, suggesting sarcastically that the city fathers should ask for two moons a month and do without street lighting altogether. Eventually Ripley whose "Believe it or Not" cartoon was syndicated throughout the world or one of his imitators, got on to it, and Stornoway's parsimony became a matter for international merriment.

The public life of the town and island was at a low ebb at that time for reasons which I will deal with later.

The strictures passed on the town by outsiders at the time of the Town Hall Pub affair were less merited. The "Scotsman" devoted more than a column to the incident in a very supercilious and sarcastic vein. The article began with a reference to "the casuists of the Lews whose dialectic wit has been sharpened by the subleties of many a theological argument."

It went on to say the citizens of Stornoway "were poor, but they were proud."

"A small modest building would not satisfy them." They tried to raise the cost of the elaborate building they erected by "assiduous mendicity" scraping money together "from all parts of the wealthy south." "Stornoway now has a beautiful Library and handsome Town Buildings. The anxieties of erection are over; but the anxiety of payment unfortunately remains. How is the debt to be cleared? Stornoway is poor, the Lews as a whole is bankrupt... The folly of local misgovernment has never been better illustrated... No doubt it was anticipated that enough could be drained from the exhaustless riches of the South to open this Municipal Temple free from debt."

It is more than three quarters of a century since some anonymous scribe on the "Scotsman" staff wrote that article, but it still infuriates me. It epitomises so completely the arrogant, patronising, smug disdain of the South towards the North which has so often been a malign influence on our affairs. It also epitomises the ignorance.

This "incubus in masonry" as the "Scotsman" termed it, this "semi-hallowed building, designed to promote the culture and higher social life of the community", was in fact intended to provide recreation rooms for thousands of visiting fishermen who came to the port in the fishing season, and for the 2500 Lewismen who were being trained in Stornoway at that time in the largest Naval Reserve Training camp in the Kingdom. For these groups, which were employed in the service of the nation as a whole, no provision at all was made from the "exhaustless riches of the South". The nation took the benefit, but left the problem on the shoulders of "poor Stornoway" and "bankrupt Lewis". Sneering at us for our pains.

48
Provost Impeached by a Bourbon

The writing of poems — or at any rate doggerel — printed as broadsheets was a common weapon in the fiery squabbles of Stornoway's public men at the turn of the century, although "The Town Hall Pub" was the only squib I know of which did an effective demolition job.

My father's scrap book contains a series of five poems — poems and counter-poems, so to speak — arising out of a row in the Harbour Commission. It might almost be described as the affair of the brothers-in-law.

The first broadside, in prose, came, oddly enough from London. From Murdoch Maciver, a brother-in-law of Aeneas Mackenzie. It accused two of the Harbour Commissioners — Provost Anderson and Bailie J. M. Morison — of maladministration and breach of trust. It alleged that they were obstructing an investigation to screen themselves from exposure. That they had browbeaten the Harbour Collector, and driven him out of his situation for daring to claim payments from them. And that the Harbour Master was in collusion with them.

"Were I present at Stornoway," wrote Maciver, "I should not hesitate to propose that the triumvirate be expelled from all the offices of trust they hold."

The broadsheet also included a snide reference to the Provost's reputation as a philanderer — "nameless and numerous relations whom perhaps the Provost was not proud of."

They certainly did not pull their punches in debate.

The first poem attacks "an elder of the N.F.C., by vulgar lips yclept the Free", and asks the question, "Where went the coin that should have gone Unto the Harbour Trust alone?" The poem was called "The Harbour Dues." Immediately there was a riposte entitled "The Harbour Deuce". The reply suggested, "It's all a guy, as has been shown, 'tis just a bit of spleen; The Brothers-in-law are working hard to get their kindred in."

A marginal note by my father identifies the brothers-in-law as John Mackenzie, William John Mackenzie, and Captain Couper. They were working for Aeneas Mackenzie who was standing for the Town Council, or the Burgh Commission, as it was at that time.

The next in the series was in the form of the programme for a "Nigger Concert", songs being assigned to the Harbour Master, Captain Thomas Morison, as "Tom Bowling" to J. M. Morison as "Longfellow" and to Anderson as "King Coal" — he was the principal coal merchant in town.

The finale, sung by all of them, to the tune of "Strolling Round the Town", runs,

"Prowling round the town,
   Doing people down,
Up to every kind of trick,
   Seeing what harbour dues can stick,
Rushing all we can,
   Nailing every sou!,
A rare old, fair old ricketty tricketty crew."

This brought a reply entitled "The Traitors", in which Aeneas Mackenzie is introduced as "An' E Ass" and William John Mackenzie as a Billy Goat.

Most of the allusions are too recondite to understand at this lapse of time, but it introduces a number of new characters on the fringe of the row identified by my father as Alexander Macdonald, painter, who also seems to have been a singer, and A. M. Macfarlane, "nicknamed Solomon."

The last in the series spreads the net even further with references to David Tolmie, the great grandfather of the present Procurator Fiscal; Kenneth Murray, a local hairdresser, and Angus Bain of the saw mill, but by this time it seems to have become all very remote from the Harbour Commission's affairs. When the ratepayers held their usual pre-election meeting, however, it all came into focus again.

Aeneas Mackenzie alleged that two of the Commissioners were in arrears with their harbour dues, but had signed the Commission balance sheet, year after year, knowing it was false. At that point he turned dramatically on the Chairman of the meeting, Provost Anderson, declaiming, "I impeach you, Provost John Norrie Anderson, and you, Bailie John Mackenzie Morison, with betraying the best interests of the town of Stornoway."

"When these gentlemen sit on the magisterial bench," he told the meeting, "they tell you that drink is no palliation for crime. They will sentence your children to prison for a paltry offence. They will brand you as criminals for taking an extra glass of grog. They have decided in this matter to pose as injured martyrs. I impeach them in your presence, and I am prepared to substantiate every word I have said."

"I defy Aeneas Mackenzie or any other man to prove that I signed these accounts with the knowledge that they were not correct," retorted J. M. Morison. "It was a revelation to me to know that no books were kept but jottings. I was not aware of this state of matters. There have been ships fathered down to me that I had nothing earthly to do with. Ships entered against me that should be put down to other people, and ships against me that I had nothing to do with except in advancing money to the masters to pay their port charges. This whole thing is a question of deficient book-keeping, and I hurl the impeachment back in Mr Mackenzie's face. A vile conspiracy has been afoot to brand honest men with dishonest motives."

Johnnie Anderson went even further. He attacked his attackers.

"It has been my experience in public life that the men who are readiest in charging their fellow men with improper actions are the men themselves that are most guilty of them."

At this point there was pandemonium in the hall. The audience yelled and cheered and protested. Aeneas and John Mackenzie stood on the platform one on each side of Johnnie Anderson, stamping, and gesticulating, and demanding a withdrawal.

"Have I the right to be heard?" demanded the Provost. "Yes" shouted the audience.

"I have said it, gentlemen. That is my experience in public life, and I repeat it."

He went on later to allege that both John Mackenzie and Aeneas Mackenzie were themselves mentioned in the auditor's report.

"That's a lie and you're a liar," shouted Aeneas, brandishing a fistful of receipts.

"That's not Parliamentary. You can keep that language for the Slip," retorted Anderson.

"I am charged with steamers for which I am not due," he continued. "The parties who are really liable are willing to pay them but Commisioner John Mackenzie says 'No. Anderson must pay.' We are hung up in a pillory, and an attempt made to discredit us in the eyes of the community, and to destroy our public career, but it will not succeed."

Alleging that Aeneas Mackenzie had pursued him for years with spite and calumny, Anderson continued, "It is said of the Bourbons that they never forgive and they never forget. Gentlemen — there sits a Bourbon!" He pointed at Aeneas adding, "I have documents in my possession that would hurl that man where he would like to hurl me. And they shall see the light of day."

After the storm Peter Macleod made a conciliatory speech. There were fourteen names on the list of those in arrears. "Do you want us to pillory these fourteen men before we hear what they have to say? I have attended all the meetings. I have gone through the auditor's report very carefully. I ask you to suspend your judgement on a good deal of what you have heard tonight — on both sides."

Having had their fun, the ratepayers thanked the speakers and the chairman, and went home to talk it over.

It was a lively town.

49

Pilot at Twelve Years Old

I was still in my pram when Aeneas Mackenzie died. I have no recollection of him, except in so far as his name reverberated through the gossip of my childhood and my youth. Inevitably it was the animosity between him and Johnnie Anderson, and J. M. Morison, that was remembered rather than what any of them did for the town. Personalities are always more interesting than principles.

Roddie Stephen recorded it all for posterity in his book about Stornoway called "Portrona", but few people now have the clue to his cryptic allusions.

Stephen, a gentle soul, who must have been appalled by the bitterness against each other of his fellow townees, wrote three poems which he described as lost cantos of Dante's "Purgatorio". They were dedicated by the "discoverer" to the people of Stornoway.

The first describes three men labouring up a hill. "not without agony. Linked hand in hand." Their punishment was that none of them could move a step without being helped, and helping, the others. When the poet asked their story one of them replied:

"Three men are we
    That lived together in a little town
Upon an island girdled by the sea
    That frets the British coast. Still meaning well,
We strove together much, and seldom found
    That right the other did, or said, or sought.
At length our long debate on earth had end;
    And each, as he passed hither, was detained
Till the others came; for only linked as one
    Could we ascend, learning what erst we scorned,
To help, not spite, each other."

Despite the animosity all three were deeply attached to the island and served it well, according to their lights.

Johnnie Anderson I have already written about and he will reappear later in various contexts. So will J. M. Morison, for a notable service to education in Lewis and for his family antecedents which are deep in the religious traditions of the island.

Aeneas, who was only 58 when he died, belonged to a well-known Lewis family, His grandfather, the Captain Ban, commanded a company in Gibraltar during the four year siege of the rock from 1779-1783, which is described in the "Encyclopaedia Britannica" as "One of the most memorable sieges of history."

Someone better equipped than I am should write the history of the part played by

Lewismen in the American War of Independence (which triggered off the siege), the French Revolutionary Wars, and the Napoleonic Wars which were all part of the same world wide shaking off of chains. It would be a remarkable story showing how closely Lewis was integrated into national affairs when it was still regarded as a remote and irrelevant backwater. Incidents from the story will arise from time to time as I proceed, but a great deal of research is required to draw the threads together, and display with accuracy the interplay of national and local affairs.

Aeneas's father has been described by another well known Lewisman, Colin Maciver, blacksmith and engineer, as "in many respects the most distinguished townsman of his day. A friend of the poor."

His name — Daniel Lewis Mackenzie — was preserved in one of the songs of my youth, about a locally built vessel, named after him. I remember only two lines, imbued with good local chauvinism:

"The D. L. Mackenzie of Stornoway Bay
    Will beat all creation when she's under way."

Aeneas himself, known as "the Balloch Mor" (to use the Stornoway spelling) was a colourful character. According to Colin Maciver, at the age of 12, he piloted a foreign vessel into Stornoway harbour, giving his orders "vociferously in good quarter deck fashion." On a sailing ship the navigation would have been complicated, but he was prompted, sotto voce, in Gaelic, by the old seaman with whom he was out fishing when they came on the foreigner.

It says something, I think, about the general relationship between town and country, Gaelic and English, at that time, that the 12-year old townee, son of a business man, was prepared to stand up and give the orders, while the much more experienced Gaelic-speaker stood in the wings — but used him, in effect, as a ventriloquist's dummy.

It also tells us something about Stornoway in the middle years of last century that Aeneas Mackenzie was educated in Daniel Stewart's College in Edinburgh.

His most important local association was with the Patent Slip which he leased from the Lewis estate in 1878, when he was 24.

"For many years afterwards," Colin Maciver records, "there was no cessation of ship-building in Stornoway, and the locally-owned fleet of merchant ships showed no signs of decadence.

"Day by day the clanging of the carpenters' mauls resounded from the harbour. In the evening coteries of carpenters and sailors were wont to frequent the pier to discuss ships and shipping and recount their vicissitudes and experiences in various parts of the world. It was not the fishing industry only which gave our harbour a busy commercial appearance in those days. There were ships coming and going continuously and sailors always congregated on our streets."

That era was only a memory by the time of the great impeachment row in the Harbour Commission. Ship-building and ship-owning had largely passed from the small ports and the local families. It was one of the first signs of a fundamental change taking place in the relationship between the centre and the periphery of an industrialised country, the effects of which we are still grappling with today.

Indeed the hostility between Aeneas Mackenzie and Johnnie Anderson may have been caused, or at any rate exacerbated, by the fact that they were jostling for elbow

146

room in a shrinking arena. There are hints in the abusive poems arising out of their quarrel that they were both in somewhat straightened circumstances because of the change in the pattern of trade.

Aeneas, according to Colin Maciver, was "the last in the long line of local shipowners" and the local ship building industry became moribund in the 1890's although occasional vessels were still slipped for repair. During the decline in shipbuilding Aeneas made an unsuccessful venture into barrel making. The huge shed which he erected for that purpose at the Slip was temporarily used for training naval reservists while the Battery of my youth, at the other end of Newton, was being built.

The Battery itself had a comparatively short life. After the Kaiser War, it became Stornoway's first Labour Exchange, situated just as inconveniently for that purpose as a building could be.

Colin Maciver records that an old sailor told him that one day, when the barrel factory was being used for training reservists, he and Aeneas watched an instructor, Sullivan to name, demonstrating the use of single-sticks. His idea of training was to give the poor recruit a thorough drubbing. Aeneas, who had a low flash point, seized the stick from the astonished instructor and gave him a drubbing instead.

On another occasion the Captain of HMS Flirt, which was stationed at Stornoway challenged the locals to a rowing match. Aeneas accepted the challenge, organised a crew, taking one of the oars himself, and left the Flirt's boat standing. Ironically the boat the locals used had been discarded as unserviceable by the Flirt on her visit the year before.

Aeneas was the leading Tory in Lewis in his day, but he was a forward-looking man. He was the first to advocate the provision of hostels for rural pupils attending the Nicolson, although it was a decade after his death before the first hostel was provided. He was also one of the founders of Lews Hospital, and for twenty years the leading figure in the Local Lodge of Oddfellows, a mysterious body about which I never knew very much although my uncle was their chaplain. They had regalia and a ritual like the Freemasons, but their primary function was mutual insurance in times of stress, and they gradually faded away with the rise of the welfare state.

Aeneas, Johnnie Anderson and J. M. Morison were all locals, although Anderson's name suggests that the family were incomers at one stage.

William Lees, the Harbour Collector at the centre of the row, was descended from one of the Fife Adventurers — the Scottish lairds sent into Lewis by James VI who had the strange delusion that it was an El Dorado waiting to be plundered, but hypocritically concealed his greed under the pretext that he was sending a civilising mission to an island where the people were "void of any knowledge of God or his religion."

Roddie Stephen, who celebrated the feuds of his fellow townsmen in his "Purgatorio", was a first generation Lewisman, son of a shipmaster from Boddam who married a descendant of the Breves — the hereditary judges of Lewis whose progeny also include the greatest of English historians, a famous modern novelist, one of the mutineers of the "Bounty", the Blind Harper of Dunvegan, the founder of the railway clearing house system, one of the leaders of Britain's anti-slavery movement, and the most notorious murderer in Lewis history who never killed anyone in his life.

147

Aspects of all these links are relevant to my examination of the process by which those of us who have been privileged to live in a real community come to understand the organism of which we are part, but they throw up so many complex patterns of recollection I must pause for breath and defer them to another volume.

My search for Lewis has hardly begun.